MW01235245

Dunamis

*Transcendent Leadership Power
for the 21st Century*

Dunamis

*Transcendent Leadership Power
for the 21st Century*

Dr. Ronaldo I. Archer

The Dunamis Institute
Maui, Hawaii

Printed in the United States of America

B C D E F G E

ISBN 0-9721311-0-8

This publication is designed to provide accurate and authoritative information with regard to the subject matter involved. It is sold with the understanding that the publisher is not engaged in rendering
legal, accounting or other professional advice. If legal advice or other expert assistance is required, the
services of a qualified professional person should be sought.

-From: A Declaration of Principles, jointly adopted by a Committee of the American Bar Association
and a Committee of Publishers and Associations.

Visit our home page at: http://www.ronarcher.com

Table of Contents

Part I—Finding Dunamis

Chapter One: Dunamis Makes You Resilient

This chapter introduces the concept of "Dunamis Resilient Quotient (RQ)," a key component of the Dunamis leader. RQ is the collection of beliefs, values, norms and traditions that affect one's attitudes, actions, and reactions to life's challenges, obstacles and failures. RQ asks the questions: do failure, pain and sorrow make you Better or Bitter, a Winner or a Whiner, a Victor or a Victim? The chapter includes a self-test that permits readers to assess their current RQ.

Chapter Two: What is Dunamis?

This chapter reviews Dunamis in an historical context and includes several examples of Dunamis leaders through the years. The character and accomplishments of such leaders are also contrasted with the morally questionable behavior of current day executives, underscoring the value of transcendent power.

Chapter Three: What is Power?

This chapter examines the nature of power, and compares Dunamis (spiritual power) and Exousia (position power). Using historical examples along with reflections drawn from personal experience, the author explains the "seven principles of the self-centered life," and contrasts them with a life lived in accordance with the principles of Dunamis.

Chapter Four: How Dunamis Will Change Your Life

This chapter explores the attributes of successful leaders (information, talent, and character), and shares the insights of several noteworthy leaders on the "secrets of success." More important, the chapter includes sensible, proven, easy-to-follow suggestions on self-improvement in all three areas of discussion.

Chapter Five: Organizational Dunamis

This chapter applies the concepts of Dunamis to the organization, and overlays them on generally accepted organizational development models. Readers will develop new insights into how to identify, work with and lead individuals who exhibited various behavioral types, and will also understand the dynamics of effective team performance.

Taken in combination, these concepts provide leaders with the insights they need to shepherd their teams through the various stages of development, and also help them get the most out of each individual on their teams. Concepts such as appreciative inquiry, organizational architecture and change management theories are introduced in this chapter. The theme of this chapter is that organizations are more like organisms and take on the personality of their leaders.

Part II – Unleashing Dunamis
Chapter Six: My Year on Ice— The Personal Dunamis Experience

Contributed by Dr. Sean Gilmore, this chapter recounts the author's own initial encounter with Dunamis and how it transformed his personal challenges into his PhD thesis. Being afflicted by Fibro Malaga and losing his father at the same time, this leader shares how he turned his scars into stars and his stumbling blocks into stones of success and achievement.

Chapter Seven: International Dunamis: Principled—Centered Leadership

This chapter, which was co-authored by Ron Archer and Dr. Aldo Fontao, explores Dunamis from an international perspective. It includes Dr. Fontao's reflections on his own experiences along with insights into Dunamis on the world stage. Dr. Aldo Fontao is a cardiologist and served as the chief of medicine for the past four presidents of Argentina. He pastored the largest church in Argentina. He is the leading international leadership development consultant in the third world. He speaks to professionals in countries in South America and Asia. He discusses his near-death experience and how it transformed his life and his leadership style.

Chapter Eight: Dunamis for Women in the 21st Century

Contributed by Dr. Danita Hughes and based on her own personal and professional experiences, this chapter explores the relationship between Dunamis and women's issues, and applies the concepts of Dunamis to the challenges faced by women in the modern world as emerging leaders.

Chapter Nine: The Dunamis Institute—Transcendent Leadership Development

This chapter serves both as a summary of the book's content and a call to action. We leave readers with a "field guide" to Dunamis, a handbook for applying the principles and the insights we explore in the book.

Acknowledgements

This book represents my promise to God, when I was sixteen years old, to some day write a book about the kind of power that transformed my life and saved me from a life of impotency and irrelevancy. There are many I must acknowledge and thank who have been angels in disguise.

Thanks go to my contributing authors, Dr. Danita Johnson Hughes, Dr. Sean Gilmore, Dr. Aldo Fontao, Cynthia Archer and Tony Garrihy who took the time and the effort to share their own Dunamis experiences in their various chapters.

I thank my mother, who, in spite of all that she endured in her life, did her best to teach me how to win and to never give up on my dreams. My mother is a unique combination of attributes: coming from very humble beginnings she forged a path for her family in a jungle laced with hidden land mines, trap-doors and hungry predators looking to devour her and her children. When weaker souls would have given up on life she thrived and survived. With her razor sharp wit, mulatto beauty and her iron will she never complained about the hand life dealt her, she just drove herself and all those around her to claim their share of the American Dream.

I must thank my aunt Cindy Paci-Hughes, my guardian angel, who has always been my model for hustle, drive and ingenuity. Growing up in a home without a father or any other male role model, Cindy created out of dirt and dust a vast real-estate empire and taught me how to take responsibility for my dreams.

Cindy, I love you so much, this book would have never happened without your undying support. When I needed a better education you paid for my tuition to attend St. Peter Chanel Catholic High School where I discovered my leadership potential, as I became the school's first Black Student Body President. When I needed a car, you made sure I got one; when I needed money while I was in college, you made sure that I got it; when I needed a job while I was in high school, you let me work as a painter for your property management company. Whenever I was down, depressed, beaten up, unsure, you were always there to make sure, somehow, I made it through. When I was 26 years old and announced my dream of building what today is a million dollar speaking, consulting, leadership development organization, you were my first and only investor. During the first lean year of my fragile business, your credit cards kept me afloat as I drove around the country building my dream. I owe a debt to you that I could never repay in two lifetimes. Thank you from the bottom of my heart.

I thank Richard Mauk for inviting me to a Christian camp when I was 15 years old, where I first heard the gospel of Jesus Christ, preached by Pastor Eddie L. Hawkins of the Good Shepard Church in Cleveland, Ohio, an experience that would forever change my life. It was neither Chanel High School that changed me, nor football: it was Dunamis.

I must also thank Mrs. Delores Mauk Ray for always taking me to church, come rain or shine, even after I made her late every Sunday.

And Rachel Mauk, who gave me the first view of how a beautiful, Godly young woman talked and acted. Your template helped me find my wife Cynthia, who shares your same Godly humility and grace.

Thanks to Sandy Stubblefield, Assistant Vice President of

Burlington Northern Santa Fe Railroad, who had the faith to let me share with the thousands of her organization's leaders, managers and supervisors the concept of Dunamis Leadership and positive organizational change.

I thank Dr. Harry Bury who taught me how to lead with love at work.

Thanks to Bruce and Michele Murphy for the wise advice of learning how to be still.

I am also indebted to Debbie and Marsha Davidson, two of the most dynamic women of our time. I am so proud of the work you both are doing with your dynamic organization, Christian Women in Action (CWA), and the thousands of lives you both have impacted for Christ with your commitment and conviction to lead retreats for Christian women. Thanks for all your love and support through the good and the bad times.

To my Pastor, Joey Johnson, you taught me how to lead with humility, love and wisdom. You are a great servant leader and I love and respect you so much. You are class and cool wrapped up in one man who can sing, preach, teach, counsel and play one mean game of racquetball. Your friendship is priceless.

To all my many friends in Nebraska: "GO BIG RED!!"

To my sister, April, the only other person on earth who speaks my secret language of cartoons: "And this time I didn't forget the gravy."

I thank John Haggai, Founder of the Haggai Institute in Singapore, for being my inspiration for the development of the Dunamis Institute.

To Jody, Carl, Lisa, Lorraine, Ronnie, Buster, Happy, Kay, Gerry, Buddy, Fanny, Allen, Tony, TT, Antuan, Steven, Ronald,

Junior, Jamie, Shauna, Monster, Dante, Keisha, Rona, Mona, Christine, Christian, Allison, Greg, John, Carlton, Ted, Tone, Donald, Kadisia, Bernice, Orlando, Craig, Tina, Harriett, Chico, Plez, Monique, Dwight, Phillip, Jason, Cedric, Chris and Ashley: I hope that this book helps you to discover, understand, embrace and unleash DUNAMIS, the power that transforms pain into power and failures into fortune.

In memory of Eleanor and Isaac.
Love always.
Skeezix

About the Authors

This book is a collaboration between several noted professionals from a variety of disciplines, who are all members of the Archer and Associates consulting firm.

Ronaldo I. Archer, Ph.D.

Ron Archer has been nicknamed "The Maestro of Motivation" by the National Speaker's Association for his ability to educate, energize, and empower his audiences.

For over fifteen years, Ron Archer has provided leadership development for professional football players in the NFL — including teams like the Cleveland Browns, Miami Dolphins and the Kansas City Chiefs. He is one of the leading national experts in the implementation of systems for the maturation of organizational effectiveness—systems for clients worldwide.

A highly sought-after speaker, Dr. Archer delivers some 180 keynote addresses a year to a wide variety of corporations and organizations. He is the author of *Ron Archer On Teams*, a guide for the implementation of high performance teams, and the co-author of "Pressure is a Privilege: The Art of Adversity Management."

A graduate of Baldwin Wallace College, Ron Archer is Chairman and founder of The Dunamis Institute, an international leadership-training firm based in Maui, Hawaii. The institute is dedicated to maximizing human potential through personal and professional development. He is the host of a national television program on the Business and Technology Network. Ron addresses over one million people per year through his various television, radio, keynote and conference appearances.

Cynthia D. Archer, M.S.

President and CEO of Archer and Associates Consulting, Cynthia is one of the most sought after experts in the application of change management using the appreciative approach. For over twelve years, Cynthia has led organizations through strategic planning retreats, team building seminars, corporate diversity roll-out plans and as a keynote speaker for Fortune 500 companies. She has her Masters Degree in Organizational Development and Analysis from Case Western Reserve University.

Danita Hughes, Ph.D.

Danita Johnson Hughes is President and Chief Executive Officer of Edgewater Systems for Balanced Living, Inc. a comprehensive human services provider located in Gary, Indiana. Prior to joining Edgewater Systems, she held various positions in the mental health and human services fields. She is also a senior consultant for Archer and Associates.

Dr. Hughes is a graduate of Indiana University with both Bachelors and Masters degrees in Public Administration. She also holds a Doctorate degree in Social Service Administration and a graduate certificate in Health Administration and Policy from the University of Chicago.

Dr. Hughes is also President of The Johnson Hughes Group, and has been certified by *The Professional Woman Network*, an international training organization specializing in professional development. She has run five marathons a year and is a dynamic motivational speaker with the Archer and Associates Speakers' Bureau.

Dr. Aldo Fontao

Dr. Aldo Fontao is a prominent cardiologist in his native Argentina, where he has been the personal physician of that country's presidents. He is widely respected in the international community for his ideas on promoting leadership in the developing world. He serves as the Vice President for Leadership Development for the Haggai Institute in Maui and as an advisor for Archer and Associates.

Sean Gilmore, Ph.D.

Dr. Gilmore is a Professor of Communications at Baldwin Wallace College, where he teaches courses in Business Communications, Persuasion and Diversity. Dr. Gilmore has consulted with numerous professionals and businesses on how to communicate more effectively.

Tony Garrihy

Tony Garrihy, the editor of Dunamis, is a speechwriter and executive coach who has consulted with numerous senior leaders, primarily in the telecommunications industry. He specializes in helping executives communicate more effectively with their key stakeholders – especially their employees— and has an outstanding record of helping companies improve organizational performance.

To book Ron Archer for a keynote speech on Dunamis please call 1-800-3-ARCHER

To Order additional copies of *Dunamis: Trancendent Leadership Power for the 21st Century*, please call 1-866-4-DUNAMS

To attend and register for a Ron Archer live public seminar please go to www.lessonsinleadership.com

To book Dr. Danita Johnson Hughes, Cynthia Archer, Dr. Sean Gilmore, Dr. Aldo Fontao, or Teresa Bower please call 440-891-0903 or go to www.ronarcher.com and fill the speaker request form on the contact us page.

Dedication

I dedicate this book to Cynthia D. Archer, my wife, my soul-mate, my best friend, my lover and the queen of my empire. You are a gift from God. You taught me how to love and how to be loved unconditionally. You are my armor bearer, my business partner, my travel buddy, my librarian and my greatest joy. May this book reflect the love, the grace and the mercy that God has always shown to us.

Love you always with the love of Christ,
Your grateful husband,
Ron

Foreword

I first met Ronaldo I. Archer when he was a student in the Behavioral Theories of Management course that I had the privilege of teaching some years ago.

At first, I thought "Ronaldo" signified a pet name similar to the Spanish "Ronaldisto," meaning "little sweet Ronald." Ron's bearing and behavior, as a college senior, however, quickly suggested otherwise. His commanding voice and demeanor conveyed leadership qualities not to be denied. Hardly "little and sweet," his tall and sturdy stature, together with an apparent self-confidence, demonstrated actual and potential leadership qualities which have ultimately blossomed into a successful career of a community leader, entrepreneur, writer and motivational speaker.

While a student, Ron's approach to academic life communicated an openness to thinking differently, with an inquisitiveness to experience how behavioral theories could empower him to become an effective leader on campus and afterwards.

I particularly remember one moment in class when Ron made a connection, which has persisted throughout his life. With him, I was conducting a role-play in managing conflict. Ron experienced the value of active listening, how through such behavior the listener, far more effectively than giving advice, can influence "the other" to think and feel differently, resulting in a peaceful, win-win resolution to the conflict. The learning: change first your own behavior before engaging the other to change.

That experience in listening and that ensuing dialogue, by his own admission, has continued to inspire Ron's vision and spark his passion in unleashing transcendent leadership power and positive organizational change.

Transcendent leadership forms the essence of the Dunamis concept, so beautifully dramatized in this book – of leading others, rather than managing others, and inspiring others, rather than directing others. And it all begins with changing ourselves.

Ron Archer, the college student and the transcendent leader, by listening, by speaking, and by being a man of action, has become the driving force behind the establishment of the Dunamis Institute on the island of Maui, in Hawaii. Here, leaders of every nation experience the joy of learning, being refreshed and realizing the transcendent power of Dunamis, it's spiritual influence for goodness and well-being in both their public and their personal lives.

I remember Ron's positive approach to life, a characteristic setting him apart from his student associates. From his youth, there existed a strong belief in a loving God. This realization later evolved into Ron's understanding that every individual, far from being defective, was endowed by God with the innate desire to add value and to be productive based on her or his unique purpose, passion and calling. This belief forms the foundation for unleashing the power of Dunamis in one's life.

Such a realization, however, did not prevail untested. In Chapter Two, Ron clearly recounts and takes responsibility for his failures, both in business and in love. In Chapter One, Ron describes how significant emotional events affected his young life. Witnessing his mother often being beaten by his stepfather, and suffering his own rejection by the only male figure in his family, it would have been easy for Ron to drift into learned helplessness, plead the victim, or simply give up. Ron's faith in

God's love for him, however, provided a glimmer of hope and gave him the power to rise from the ashes. Ron knows, from experience, how to fail, how to make a mess of his life, despite all his potential. No individual can complain that Ron has no idea what she or he is going through. Ron's been there, done that. Ron also knows from experience how to make a success out of his life and still be bereft of happiness. Money, fame, success did not fill the emptiness of his soul. He knows that the greater the gifts a leader possesses, the greater risk for him or her to fall into the trap of narcissism and self-worship.

More importantly, Ron now knows and can help us all to know how to heal the brokenness in our own lives; how to become better, not bitter, and how not to give up!

The journey begins with a ruthless self-examination, a journey inward, as he explains in this book. It continues with a successful navigation of one's life in response to pain, wounds and failures through a humble and grateful faith in God. No pollyannist, Ron has lived the bitterness of life and come through it all to experience the promised land, the gift of Dunamis-love, joy, peace, patience, kindness, goodness, faithfulness, humility and discipline as we interface with one another – a genuine transformation of ourselves and our organizations. Read this book! It is an event in which the student has clearly outdone his teacher. As his professor and a Roman Catholic priest, I have benefited immensely from Ron's spirit and reflections. I have learned, among other things, to accept my own frailties and the exigencies of life, while not getting stuck in my own self-pity.

So, I urge you to read this book in its entirety. You'll like it! Better yet, you'll think and feel differently. It may even empower you to change your life and become the transcendent leader you have the potential to become.

Professor Harry J. Bury, Ph.D.
April 21, 2002

Preface

This book is for those who are serious about experiencing the effects of extraordinary power in their lives as leaders, spouses, parents, pastors, public servants, coaches and entrepreneurs. If you want to receive the miraculous and unleash the supernatural, then you want DUNAMIS, the Transcendent Power for the 21st Century. Dunamis transforms pain into power, wounds into wisdom, misery into ministry, hate into love, battling bosses into collaborative coaches and casual involvement into personal commitment.

A Brief Summary

This book is about the kind of leaders, workers, parents that people in the world hunger for. We crave leaders, lovers, and friends who possess a high "**Resiliency Quotient**", a high "**Information Quotient**", a high "**Talent Quotient**" and a high "**Character Quotient**." Organizations everywhere are searching for people who are more like thermostats than thermometers, leaders who do not take polls before every decision, teachers who are not afraid to lead with faith, love and conviction, coaches who listen and empower with integrity and compassion.

We cry out, "Where are the next Martin Luther Kings, the next Billy Grahams, the next Mother Teresas?" Put another way, "What has happened to Transcendent Power?"

If you know what to look for, such power is out there, flowing with the Spirit of love, joy, peace, patience, kindness, goodness, faithfulness, humility and self-control. Transcendent Power is accessible. The question is, "Are you ready to receive it and unleash it to transform your world?" When the student is ready, the teacher will appear.

In the movie *The Matrix*, Morpheus, the teacher, (Lawrence Fishburne) is preparing Neo, the student, (Keanu Reeves) to come to grips with the reality that he, Neo, is the "One"—the one who will take on the evil forces within the Matrix and bring it to its knees. As with anyone being told he is the one to save mankind from evil, Neo is having a hard time swallowing the hype.

During his training, Neo must follow Morpheus and jump from the rooftop of one skyscraper to another, a distance of 50 yards. Morpheus tells Neo, "I want to free your mind. Don't **think** you can, **know** you can. Walking the path and knowing the path are two different things."

Neo watches Morpheus run and leap from one rooftop to the next, like a flying squirrel leaping from one tree branch to another. All Neo can say in shock and wonderment is, "Whoa!!!"

If you are tired of tired platitudes, worn out clichés and antiquated, narcissistic five-step plans that get the same results year after year, I dare you to take a quantum leap and read this book. This book is going to introduce to some and present to all the most awesome leadership principle in the universe today: a power so great it will turn whiners into winners, quitters into climbers, chumps into champs and pretenders into contenders. We are going to study the ancient Greek concept of transcendent power called **Dunamis** and compare it with what the ancient Greeks would call *Exousia*, or "**Executive Power**"— the kind of modern power that we today would call "position power" . We are going to define your **Resiliency Quotient** (RQ), which has a direct impact on your **Information Quotient** (IQ), **Talent Quotient** (TQ) and **Character Quotient** (CQ), which all leads to what I call "Unleashing Dunamis."

We are going to discover how to use Dunamis to change ourselves first, and then the world around us. We will identify the five stages of organizational transcendent transformation and the three groups that emerge as we grapple with the process of change. I call these three groups the Winners, the Whiners and the Wanderers.

This book is not for the faint-hearted or the closed-minded. If you want to stay in the Matrix and drift along in a world of uninspired and impotent leadership, then take the blue pill and close this book now! Don't you dare read another page.

If you are ready to shed the Clark Kent suit of mediocrity and put on the red cape of Dunamis, read on. If you are ready to leap from challenge to challenge, slaying Goliaths, crossing Red Seas, and bringing dead, dry-boned organizations back to life, then take the red pill. This book is for you. Dunamis will help you astound your employees and astonish your customers, leaving them both saying a single word: Whoa!

This book will help you plug into the most awesome leadership force known to humankind: a transcendent power that will turn your world upside down, and take you on a wild roller-coaster ride of influence and change. Read on and we will travel to a dimension of power that will forever change your life and the lives of those around you.

The question for you is: "How badly do you want transcendent power?" You have to really want it. When you get sick and tired of being sick and tired, sick of going to meetings where

minutes are kept and hours are lost, sick of organizations confusing activity with accomplishment, where leaders act like blind
dogs in darkened rooms chasing black cats that are not there,
then you are ready for Dunamis.

Dunamis Must Be Breathed In

A lost young man traveling in a strange land stumbled upon
an old man sitting next to a barrel of water. Above the old man
was a sign that read, "Behold, Here Sits The Wisest Man On
Earth: you are allowed to ask him one question." He approached
the old man, who had a weather-worn face and a long white
beard, and asked, "What is the secret of life?

The old man took the young man and asked him, "Look
deeply into the water in the barrel." As the young man stared
into the water's mirror-like reflection, he asked the old man,
"What am I looking for?" It was then that the old man grabbed
the young man's head and held it under the cold, icy water.
After a minute, he lifted the young man's head out of the water
and asked him, "What do you want?" The young man cried
out, "The secret of life." The old man held his head under the
water a little longer, lifted his head out of the water and asked
the young man a second time, "What do you want?" The young
man cried out again, "The secret of life." For the third time the
old man held the young man's head under the water for what
seemed to be at least four minutes. The young man, near
drowning and his hands frantically slapping and scratching the
old man's arms, nonverbally begged to be released him from
death's grip. Finally, the old man let him up and asked him,

"What do you want?" The young man, gasping and choking, screamed out, "Air!" Then the old man said, "When your desire to obtain Dunamis is as much as your desire to breathe, then and only then will you be ready to be filled with the transcendent power that is the secret to life."

Introduction

Dunamis

The days of "command and control" leadership are passing. People in all walks of life long for visionary leaders who lead with transcendent power, passion, humility, goodwill and love. Leaders today must be able to project themselves as human beings and not human doings, leaders who connect with the mind, soul and spirit. People are in search of significance and will offer their voluntary commitment only to those leaders who make them feel important and valued.

The events of September 11, 2001, demonstrated to the entire world the undeniable value of transcendent leaders. In the midst of an unprecedented national tragedy, one man, New York Mayor Rudolph Giuliani, was a tower of strength for the people of his city – and indeed the people of our nation. During this trying period, Giuliani – who had long been viewed as a proto-typical autocratic "command and control" manager — was able to tap an inner source of spiritual strength, and the results were astonishing: the hard-boiled Giuliani was revealed to us anew as a feeling, compassionate, and soulful leader. His leadership demonstrated a wonderful blend of efficiency and spirit, touching both the mind and the heart. Not only did he bring order out of chaos, he brought hope out of despair.

The ancient Greeks called this power of spiritual leadership **Dunamis**, and held it in higher regard than the power that came from one's position or station in life, which they called **Exousia**.

Employees today are simply too well educated – and often

are too cynical – to respond to exousia leaders who offer compliance, not commitment. To get the most out of such employees, organizations of all kinds need visionary leaders who can connect with people on a spiritual and emotional plane – leading them rather than managing them, inspiring them rather than directing them.

In short, today's organizations need Dunamis Leaders.

This book explains the concept of Dunamis leadership — including its historical roots and its present-day manifestations – and explains Dunamis leadership in the context of current theories of industrial and organizational psychology.

Using practical examples of Dunamis in action, we posit a new leadership model that is capable of transforming individuals and organizations, taking both the leader and his or her team to remarkable new heights of personal effectiveness and performance excellence.

Most of the concepts the authors present in Dunamis have been incorporated into Ron Archer's keynote presentations, national television programs, consulting assignments and executive coaching clinics. These concepts have created a great deal of positive feedback from the hundreds of thousands of individuals who have attended these sessions. Moreover, our consulting work with numerous businesses and non-profits suggest profound interest in a values-based and spiritually driven leadership system like Dunamis. Church leaders, political leaders, business executives and educators are standing in line to order Ron's new book on Dunamis. He has been teaching the subject for the past three years and the demand for a written record of Dunamis leadership is extraordinarily high.

The book is written for professionals at all levels of an organization who wish to lead their teams to superior levels of performance, while attaining higher levels of personal satisfaction and employee satisfaction. While this book is written from a decidedly Christian perspective, it will be of interest and value to anyone interested in understanding – and harnessing — the spiritual dimension of the leadership dynamic. Dr. Martin Luther King, Jr. used Dunamis to challenge the soul of a nation; Mother Teresa used Dunamis to love and care for the unwanted and the unloved; Princess Diana used Dunamis to give the royal crown a humane face and touch. Nelson Mandela used Dunamis to change the course of South African History.

Like many best-selling, self-help/personal improvement books, this book is built around principles that the reader will readily identify with, and which are easy to understand and act upon. This is especially true of readers who proceed from a Judeo-Christian worldview.

The book is written in a straightforward and conversational tone that makes it extremely approachable and readable. Readers will find it easy to grasp and act upon the ideas and suggestions in this book, and will be greatly affected by their life-changing potential. Many who hear Ron Archer in person or on television will be excited to know that his book reads with the same passion and conviction that has made him one of the most sought-after motivational speakers in the world today.

Chapter **1**

Dunamis Will Make You Resilient

"Weeping may endure for a night, but Joy comes in the Morning"

Your **Resiliency Quotient (RQ)** impacts and enhances two areas of your life:

The first area RQ impacts is the collection of beliefs, values, norms and traditions that affect your attitudes, actions and reactions to life's challenges, obstacles and failures. RQ asks the question, "Does failure, pain and sorrow make you Better or Bitter, a Winner or a Whiner, a Victor or a Victim?" What do you do when the bottom of life drops out from under you. You are left hanging by your blessed assurance, hoping it holds.

Second, RQ can be used as a simple method of evaluating one's ability to handle the vicissitudes of life. It measures how effectively you counter the unexpected and the unforeseen trials and tribulations of life with a spirit of peace, love, kindness, goodness, joy, faithfulness, humility, patience and discipline.

Let's examine the first area.

An ancient Jewish proverb states, "As a man believes in his heart, so he becomes." In other words, you are what you believe, and your beliefs shape your destiny. Beliefs are so powerful that they create historical movements, political revolutions and even independent countries. As Dr. Martin Luther King, Jr. said, "Either we stand for something, or fall for anything." Beliefs order our lives and define our capabilities.

A strong resiliency quotient can positively change your beliefs, perceptions, ideals, talents and character. If developed and nurtured, your RQ will be the most meaningful and lasting attribute that you will ever posses.

A strong RQ will forever change your life, work and destiny. A strong RQ affirms certain immutable truths that are universally held by Dunamis leaders.

Dunamis teaches you that weeping may endure for a night, but that joy comes in the morning. All of us have spent sleepless nights dwelling on our broken dreams, shattered hopes and painful setbacks. Yet if we understand the Dunamis concept that all things work together for the good for those that love God and for those that are called to act according to His purpose, then we can rest easy knowing that there is a positive lesson to be learned from every difficult situation.

We all have a story to tell. I know what it means to be ashamed—wanting to hide the truth about your background. Shame is a powerful prison to be trapped in: it spreads to your children, to your spouse and to your business...

Before you read the next section, I need to explain some things about my relationship with my mother. First, my mother is a very proud, strong and resourceful woman who has overcome tremendous vicissitudes to get to her place in the sun. As a single parent, she was an excellent provider and she tried her best to give me the greatest chance to earn my share of the American

Dream. She made sure my younger sister and I had great Christmas holidays and joyous birthdays. She taught me how to win and to never to settle for second best…but to always aim for the stars. She stressed the value of education and how important it was in order to achieve the American Dream. Her greatest gift to me was the *Child Craft Encyclopedias* that I read every single day. It started me on the road to knowledge and wisdom.

When I was the keynote speaker before an audience of 5,000 at an international conference in Texas, I flew her down to be with me. I called her on stage and gave her two dozen roses. During my first national television show on the Business Technology Network, I brought her on the set and recognized her as being a significant person in my life.

Life for her was no crystal staircase. But out of respect for her privacy, I will not share in this body of work her own child-hood and the events associated with it.

But in order to help the thousands I have met and talked to across the country, who have been deeply wounded and scarred, I must share with them the power that Dunamis can have in healing our brokenness and reviving our wayward souls.

Mom, I love you and I know if my story can save just one person from a life of shame, self-hate and misery that it would make all that you and I have gone through worth it. God spared us both to encourage others who may be living in quiet desperation, not knowing the freedom and hope available to them through Dunamis. To God Be the Glory!

The End of Innocence and the Beginning of Shame

I was about five years old when I was introduced to a world

of shame and dysfunctionality. A woman, who my mother trusted as a baby sitter, sexually molested both my best friend and me. The things she did to us cannot be detailed in this book for it would offend decent sensibilities. I remember feeling "not just right ever again." I felt damaged, used and off-balance. I felt like a ghost who was there, but not really there. The babysitter said this was our very special secret and we never told anyone. She put our hands in places where young boys hands should not be on a grown woman's body. She made us "play with each other." She fondled and touched us in places where young boys should not be touched. This woman robbed me of my innocence by making me sexually aware and active before any child should be. While most kids were thinking innocent thoughts, my mind had been polluted with images and feelings that would haunt me the rest of my life.

When our family moved out of the Green View Apartments in the inner city of Cleveland, into an urban, blue collar neighborhood called Lee and Harvard, I became the most sexually active five year old anyone had ever seen. For me being sexually aware and active was as normal as playing football, wrestling and "tag, you are it."

I remember trying to have "real sex" at age five with one of my girlfriends. We went behind her garage and I showed her what had been taught to me by my babysitter. Thank God, this poor girl's parents caught us before anything happened.

It is very difficult for a man to admit that he has been the object of sexual abuse by a woman. It just does not make a man feel very manly to admit that he was molested at all. I was so messed up that, as a teenager, I ran up my mom's phone bill calling sex hotlines. I needed to talk to older women who were like my babysitter. I was always attracted to older women: women who were kind, fast, aggressive, sexually daring. My first girl-friend was a woman who was a twenty six-year-old college profes-sor and I was her fourteen-year-old man-child. I was so advanced in my knowledge of the female body that only an older woman could satisfy my level of experience and need.

By the grace of God I avoided becoming a rape victim by a friend of the family.

My mom's best friend was a woman who had three kids of her own, two girls and a boy, and two foster sons whose natural mother committed suicide. To help her with the five kids, she took in a young man she met at a Jehovah's Witnesses' meeting, who, in exchange for room and board, became her live-in male nanny. It was like putting a fox in the hen house. This guy was a predatory child molester, who lusted after preteen boys. He was very open about his homosexuality. He was what we would today call, "flaming." He wore tight, leather, black pants, had bright orange-red hair and acted very feminine. As kids, he was just funny to us. The way he laughed with a loud high-pitched gig-gle, and the way he sobbed, as he would watch his soap operas, was so funny to us. We were young and didn't really understand what it really meant to be homosexual. He had this weird crush on the actor who played Starsky on the hit TV show *Starsky and Hutch*. He had over 15 posters of Starsky in his room. He had Starsky T-shirts and a miniature model of the car that Starsky drove on the television show.

He lived up in the attic of the house and, when it was time for us to go to bed at night, all the boys slept upstairs with him. So, it was bedtime and we all climbed up the squeaky old wooden stairs to the hot musty attic.

Now, after being molested by a female babysitter, my guard was up big time and I was suspicious of anybody, especially a grown man, who says, "Let's take off all of our clothes, get oiled up like body builders and play Roman wrestle in the bed." Listen folks, I was born at night, but not last night.

To my shock and amazement, though, all three of the boys and the man got naked and all jumped into bed to play "wrestle." He would oil up his naked body and oil up their naked bodies so that they could have an orgy. This grown man was slipping and sliding all over those innocent three boys.

I had seen wrestling before and what he was doing to those boys was a form of wrestling I had never seen. I told them I had to go the bathroom and I would be right back. I ran downstairs, flabbergasted, and I stayed awake all night in my clothes, sitting in an easy chair in the living room, just thinking about what I had witnessed: how a man could do what he was doing to boys! I knew from experience that a woman could molest boys, but not a man. I was speechless about what I saw and I never told anyone. I didn't know what to say. It was surrealistic and bizarre. I never wanted to spend another night over at that woman's house, even though she was my mom's closest friend.

Two of the three boys who had been sexually abused stabbed to death the family dog. Eventually they committed suicide. Who knows the horrors those boys experienced night after night when forced to play Roman oil wrestling with their live-in male rapist?!

I never understood how my Mom's friend could let this man sleep with and raise her boys. If I, as a kid, could see that he was strange, I know they, as adults, had to see it.

I liked the lady of the house, but the male nanny was a

predator. The problem was he liked me a lot. I was his type. I was quiet, shy, soft and chubby with a sweet, wanting-to-please personality. He would always find a way to rub up against me, then he would giggle. I hated it. He was like a dog in heat chasing his prey with a laser-like focus. I didn't quite understand it then, but looking back he was constantly flirting with me, trying to seduce me. I was new, fresh meat: the only boy he had yet to violate. It was like being a long-tailed cat trapped in a rocking chair contest—I had to always protect my tail.

We were all boys without fathers, who were starved for attention from a father figure, and he used that need as a means for seduction. He was a very religious Jehovah's Witness teacher and would always talk about the story of Jonathan and David in the Bible—two men who loved each other more than brothers—to justify his love for us. This is why I speak out. I was spared so I could share my experience with others, who may be hiding a deep pain and who may be contemplating some horrible solution to their silent suffering. On behalf of those two innocent boys, who are no longer here to speak, I speak for them. I cry for them. I am witness to their suffering at the hands of a fox who was allowed to lurk and thrive in the shadows of secrecy. Parents, please be careful who you allow to be alone with your children. Many parents do a good job of protecting their daughters, but not their sons. So many young black boys are without fathers and black mothers want so desperately to find them male role models, not realizing that these same role models are predators. They use youth activities as a canvassing to pick up new fatherless boys looking to be loved by a father figure. Some, in the community, called those boys (the ones who were molested) "crazy." Of course it was wrong and appeared bizarre to kill their dog, but did anyone ask why they flipped out? These were innocent kids. It is unfortunate that some dysfunctional parents are great at blaming their children for being victims of rape, incest and molestation.

God forbid, not on my watch! As long as I have breath in my lungs, I will speak out in behalf of the silent sufferers of sexual abuse. It is time for the walls of Jericho to come tumbling down. I am tired of protecting the image and reputation of grown people at the expense of suffering children—who live out their lives in quiet desperation. If you suspect that a child is being sexually abused there is a toll free number that you can call anonymously. The number is 1-800-4-A-Child.

Dunamis, the Healing of Our Dysfunctional Past

What I have learned from my childhood is that there are no perfect parents, because there are no perfect people. All parents are wounded human beings. The pain that is created in all of our souls cannot be filled with the love of any human being. If I had perfect parents, I would still be dysfunctional in some way. It is called the effects of sin. As King David wrote, "In sin did my mother conceive me."

That's why the Apostle Paul wrote to Corinth, "We have this treasure in clay vessels that the **Excellency** of the power may be of God and not of us." Anything good that comes out of our lives is because of the grace and the mercy of God. We are all wounded souls and only the love of God can free us from our human misery.

What and who I have become is because of God's mercy and grace. It is His love that is keeping me sane in an insane world. God spared me and healed me so that I can remind my clients that God sends all of us through something, to something, to become someone who serves God and humanity. In spite of our imperfect parents, dysfunctional families, sexual abuse, rejection and shame, God can take our torn lives and make of them robes of righteousness and honor.

We have come over on different ships, but we are in the same boat now. We either learn to work together as friends, or perish as fools—for a high tide can raise all of our ships. Our races may be different, our genders, our social economic status and our religions, but what makes all of us brothers and sisters is that all of us have a story to tell. All of us have, at one time or another, lived in the shadows of shame with a secret. Much of the hate, crime, abuse and craziness in this world comes from people who have become bitter, resentful and angry about the hell they endured as children: silent suffering, quiet hurt and mute moaning.

We have a choice now with the power of Dunamis to be better, and not bitter. Yes, you were hurt; yes you were abused; yes you were raped; yes you were rejected, but you no longer have to be a victim and a prisoner of your past.

Thank God for Dunamis, which heals the rejected, the scarred, the least of these and the overlooked. I have learned that God chooses to use greatly those in life who have been wounded very deeply. Listen, my friends we are all wounded; so you are not alone. Cry out to God, scream out to a pastor, to a friend, that you are worthy of love, acceptance, blessing and happiness. Forgive those that have hurt you so that you can be set free from the bondage of hate and resentment.

Face the pain, face the hurt, emote the sorrow and then let

go so you can grow.

God wants to use your pain to heal others. I need you, the world needs you, so don't let your pain and shame keep you on the sidelines on the physically unable to perform list. We need your talent, your gifts, your ideas and your dreams to be shared. It is never too late to begin anew, every second is a new opportunity to rise, take up your bed and walk. Out of misery is where you will find your ministry. A lotus flower grows in the deepest mud, the stars shine in darkest sky, and your ministry will develop out of your greatest misery. A few examples to jump-start your heart:

- Pablo Picasso, a poor student in elementary school, was often punished by being sent to "the cell": a room where he sat on a bench isolated from the other students for being so stupid. He used his time in solitary isolation to draw—drawing non-stop. Later he became the most famous and innovative painter of the 20th Century.

- Paul Orfalea, a dyslexic who failed second grade, was erroneously put in the school for the mentally retarded for six weeks. Paul Orfalea, nicknamed Kinko after his red Afro haircut, went on to found Kinko's, the most successful photocopy chain in the United States.

- Benjamin Franklin flunked out of school and ran away to Philadelphia. As a boy, Ben Franklin taught himself algebra, geometry, navigation, grammar, logic, French, German, Italian, Spanish and Latin. As an adult, he founded the Pennsylvania Gazette, published Poor

Richard's Almanac, proved that lightning is electricity, invented bifocal lenses, founded the University of Pennsylvania, served as minister to France and signed the Declaration of Independence and the United States Constitution.

- Carly Fiorina, a UCLA Law School drop out, worked as a Hewlett-Packard Shipping Clerk. She was appointed chief executive officer of Hewlett-Packard in 1999 and became the first female CEO of a blue chip company.

- John Amos was a running back for the Denver Broncos for only 24 hours before being cut from the team. He was later dropped by another 12 professional football teams, including the Kansas City Chiefs. In spite of failure after failure he tried his hand at acting. Rejected time and again, he finally got his break as Gordy, the Weatherman of the *Mary Tyler Moore Show*, followed by James Evans on *Good Times* and finally as the adult Kunta Kinte in the most watched program in television history, *Roots*.

- Charles Thornton was abandoned by his mother and father at 3 months. He grew up around violence, drug abuse and gang activity. Close relatives went to jail, were shot and killed. In spite of his pain, rejection and hurt he decided within himself he wanted to transcend his environment. He was raised by his grandparents and lived in poverty without indoor plumbing or other modern conveniences. Later in life he enlisted in the U.S. Air

Force and worked hard to excel. Today, at age 37, he is the superintendent of personnel for Air Force One—the 747 that carries the President of the United States of America. Congratulations, Charles! You have come a long way: from the Outhouse to the White House.

* * *

Just recently, at one of my seminars on leadership, a young manager walked up to me in tears and gave me a hug, thanking me for sharing my life story. She said that my openness about my life and how God used my misery for my ministry forever changed her life. She shared a secret which had kept her stuck for years, making her feel unworthy of love and success. She shared that she was the product of her mother being raped. She always felt that she had no value because she was the product of something awful. When I said that God uses greatly those who have been wounded very deeply, it gave her hope that God could use a person with such a painful secret.

All I needed was a form-fitting CRUTCH

    C *hrist*
    R *isen*
    U *nleashes*
    T *ruth,*
    C *ourage,*
    H *ealing*

Some critics have asked me, "Aren't you using GOD as a crutch?" My response is always the same: "A crutch is what you need when you have been wounded and have a limp that won't leave. It makes sense to give a person with a broken or amputated leg a crutch; we don't question it because the need is obvious. But how about a person with a broken soul or a disabled spirit? What do we offer that person? How many around us have broken and wounded spirits and, because we don't visibly see the limp right away, we offer them nothing as they live in quiet desperation."

Do you know how many people are in need of a crutch, but are afraid to admit that they are crippled or that they have been wounded? We, as leaders, parents and coaches have to make it safe for people to share themselves with us, to be real, to be honest—we need to stop shooting our wounded.

Thank God I have a crutch that is faithful, dependable, awesome and powerful—a crutch that says weeping may endure for a night, but Joy comes in the morning; a crutch that says I have never seen the righteous forsaken or his seed begging for bread; a crutch that says all things work together for the good for those that love God and are called to His divine purpose.

Yes, I may be dysfunctional. I may be too fat and may be too black. I may cry too loud and limp too slow. I may be crippled, but I am limping to glory, dancing for joy, and like Paul, running my race and finishing my course because God has a crutch called "grace," a crutch called "mercy," a crutch called "hope," a crutch called "favor," a crutch called "providence" and a crutch called "deliverance"—all of which provide healing. If my God can use a messed up, crippled "man-child" like me, I know He can use you. I know He can be a crutch for your limp, too.

All you need do is get down on your face, like I once did, and cry out to God. Admit that you are crippled by a secret that no one else knows. Admit you have a limp that won't leave. Admit you need His divine help. Admit you need His love, and wait for the Dunamis to be released in your life.

God only gives crutches to the needy, to the humble, to the broken, to the lost, to the wounded, to the bruised and to the disturbed. Cry out to him and he will help you through and sustain you along life's journey. Humble yourself under the mighty hand of God, and He will lift you up. Isn't that what a crutch does—doesn't it lift us up and offer support?

What saved me was God's Dunamis, which He poured into my soul once I quit trying to get from my mother what I could only get from Him. That's why Jesus said: "When your mother and father forsake you, the Lord will take you up." He is a friend that sticks closer than a brother or a sister.

Give God your pain, he will make it power. Give God your misery, and he will make it ministry. Give God your wounds, He will make them wisdom. And give God your life, and He will make it a blessing to others who have been crippled by life.

Give it all to God, just like the young boy who gave Jesus all he had: two fish and five loaves of bread. The offering seemed to be too small to feed 5,000 men and an uncounted number of women and children. It wasn't the size of the gift that mattered. It was the size of the heart. That little boy gave Jesus all he had, and God took it and SUPERSIZED IT. If you are willing to give God your little talent, your small offering, your pint-sized gift, your petite potential, He will SUPERSIZE IT.

Little becomes much when placed in the Master's hand. The power is not in our talent, not in our skills, not in our good looks, but in the majesty of the anointed presence of God that takes the small and feeds all. You can't. But God can, if you let go and quit trying to do things your way.

Aren't you tired of doings things your way? How many times does life have to knock you down before you will let go? It's like the monkey who gets trapped by the zookeeper. The zookeeper places a jar on the ground and puts a shiny piece of tin foil in the bottom of the jar. The monkey sees the jar with its shiny contents, he puts his hand in the jar to grab the tin foil, but with his hand in a fist, he cannot remove it from out of the mouth of the jar. In order to get his hand out and make an escape he has to let go of his shiny, glittering prize. When the zookeeper returns to his simple trap, he finds the monkey exhausted from trying to get his hand and his prize out of the jar. The monkey is now an easy catch and is transported to the zoo cage for the rest of his days.

How many of us are in bondage to some shiny piece of junk that is keeping us in a cage? All that glitters is not gold. God may be asking you today, "Choose this day whom you will serve: the gift or the giver of the gift." That's why Jesus said: "Seek ye first the Kingdom of God and His righteousness and all these things will be added unto you."

I was a fourteen-year-old kid who accepted Jesus Christ as my personal Savior through the love of a neighbor named Delores Mauk-Ray—who picked me up, rain or shine, to take me to church every Sunday. Yes, I wet the bed, I stuttered, I was overweight, but I refused to become a quitter. Because I stuttered, at times, kids in my school had a poem about me. The poem was: "His name is Renardo, he is a retardo, he sits on the steeple, and when he talks he spits at the people."

* * *

I read the Bible and found hope in two verses that gave me confidence and hope:

"If God is with you, who can be against you?"
AND
"Things that seem impossible with man are possible with God."

I was so touched by these two passages that I began reading the Bible into a tape recorder, overemphasizing my words. I was determined to speak well, and to be a preacher, to help others who were like me.

After I accepted Jesus Christ as my Savior, I stopped stuttering, stopped wetting the bed and began to workout to lose that baby fat. I became the student body president of my high school, which was 90% white and 10% black. I won the election by a landslide. During the campaign I talked about how faith, family and fortitude were the keys to long-term success. I spoke from my soul about the Fatherhood of God and the brotherhood of Man.

I shared how my relationship with Jesus Christ had given me a power and a confidence to be able to lead as a servant. After the election, I felt a change come over me, and I prayed that one day God would allow me to share the power of love and grace with others who, like me, were "one of the least of these."

At the age of 16, Dunamis had given me a set of core values and a preferred future state. Those core values were:

- Faith in God
- Good Education
- Hard Work
- In America it is not where you start; it is where you dream you can be.

* * *

My friends, all of us have a story to tell. You have yours. Unlike mine, maybe you knew both your parents and you lived in an upper-class community. Perhaps your wound revolves around a father who was a work-a-holic or an alcoholic, a father who never told you that he loved you, never hugged or made you feel special so that today, as a parent, you don't know how to show emotion to your own children. You want to; but you feel awkward and avoid it. All of us have stories that we never share because of shame and embarrassment. Never be embarrassed again, for the truth will set you free.

This book represents the fulfillment of a promise that I made to God when I was 16: that one day I would share with the world the joy, love, peace and power that one can find in an intimate relationship with the Almighty. I would fulfill His vision of Faith through my dysfunctional life. I would tell the world how God turned my misery into ministry, my pain into power, my wounds into wisdom and my scars into stars.

Later, in the next chapter, I will explain how, on the way to writing this book, I left the RQ principles that I learned at the Good Shepard Baptist Church under Pastor Eddie Hawkins and the faithfulness of Mrs. Mauk and, like the prodigal son, lost my way for a few years. As I discovered, the good news is it is never too late to return home. God is always waiting, with open arms, to welcome us home. The key to getting back home is to be humble, pray for wisdom and direction, seek God's highest truth—which is love—and to turn from the evil that has you in bondage. Let go of the shiny tin foil in the jar. Once you let go of it, you are free to be used by God to perform miracles in your organization, miracles in your business, miracles in your ministry and miracles in your marriage. When you let go of your ego, pride and self-sufficiency, then you will be able to sing in the words of that old Negro spiritual: "Free at last, free at last, thank God Almighty, I am free at last." When you can overcome the fear of losing everything, then you are free to become almost anything. Let go of the tin foil in the jar.

Chapter *2*

What is Dunamis?

Isn't electricity amazing? You can't really see it, but you know when it is working. You also know when it has been turned off. Imagine going to your local appliance store to purchase the latest refrigerator on the market. The new wonder fridge is awesome. It can make homemade ice cream automatically. It has a dispenser for making cappuccino and espresso. It has a built-in mini-microwave, toaster and hot butter dispenser. You buy it and have it delivered to your home. You go grocery shopping and buy all the ingredients you need to pour into the homemade ice-cream dispenser. You buy steaks for the freezer and coffee beans for the built-in espresso unit. You pour and pack everything into it. You are in a hurry because you have to catch a plane for a weeklong business conference. After a weeklong series of meetings, you arrive back home and can't wait to get a cold bowl of homemade ice cream. You walk in and an awful stench hits your nose as you enter the door. You run through the house opening every window to air out the nauseating smell. You quickly discover that your new fridge is the source of the stink, and find a gooey, pasty liquid oozing out of your ice-cream maker. All your meat has spoiled and the smell is just awful.

You realize that in your hurry to catch the plane, you forgot to plug in the appliance. With all of its features, without the power source it was completely useless. In fact, it caused more of a mess than a convenience. No cold, creamy ice cream, just a messy, all-night cleaning job ahead and the tossing of five hundred dollars worth of meat, milk and ice cream ingredients.

How many leaders are trying to be agents of change without being plugged into the power source? Programs spoil, plans rot, and people work in the dark, awaiting a vision to follow. The stench smells up the entire department and the organization has to spend time cleaning mess after mess.

The resume lists all the necessary credentials and attributes. The leader went to the right school, joined the right clubs, and has all the right connections. But someone forget to plug the leader into DUNAMIS, the power source for life-changing leadership. The Enron fiasco is a good example of the kind of organizational meltdown that occurs when leaders are not equipped with the moral force that is Dunamis.

How did twelve quitters, whiners, doubters and cowards become the Dunamis leaders who forever transformed the world? These twelve misfits, along with a midget named Zachias and a reformed prostitute named Mary, would take on the greatest military power in the world and transform it from a pagan empire into a devoted Christian state. A pagan empire that crucified, beheaded, whipped, stoned, burned and fed to the lions all those who professed to believe in the vision and values of the Christos.

You thought *you* faced opposition to your new strategic plan and vision. These men and women were not very educated, talented, gifted or dynamic. For the most part, they were plain, ordinary, everyday folks. They were not people of great distinction, wealth or power. They did not hold positions of authority or prominence: no titles, or degrees; no reserved parking spaces, or plush offices. Yet somehow they were able to turn pain into power, wounds into wisdom, scars into stars and rejections into results. People who once hated them began to follow them. They became leaders of the fastest growing and most enduring movement the world had ever seen.

In the first day of operations after their "IPO," 3,000 new followers and investors decided to commit. Imagine getting 3,000 new customers in one day, or increasing and sustaining profits by 3000%. How did they do it? What did they have? Wouldn't you love to know what kind of leadership training class they attended that gave them the kind of power to turn their enemies into empowered co-workers and their foes into followers?

They, who were once afraid, timid and cowardly, were now brave, bold and dynamic. They, who once denied knowing their leader, were now publicly aligning themselves with a vision that would bring certain persecution and death. They had no swords or armies, no political lobby or inside connections, no great family name or influential friends. All they had was a supernatural power that allowed them to become Dunamis leaders who changed the world at an astonishing pace.

The Meaning Of "Dunamis"

The word "Dunamis" is first found in the Bible, in the New Testament, in the Book of Acts 1:8, as the resurrected Jesus addresses his disciples before his ascension into Heaven:

*"And you shall receive **power** (Dunamis) when the Holy Spirit is come upon you and you shall be witnesses unto me first in Jerusalem, Judea, Samaria and the uttermost parts of the world" Acts 1:8*

Jesus was preparing His disciples for a special kind of power that they would receive on the Day of Pentecost that would enable them to take on the world's greatest pagan empire and transform it into a Christian society.

The Disciples had spent three and a half years with Jesus in his ministry. They watched Him heal the lame, cure the sick, feed 5000 with a few loaves and fish, walk on water, cast out evil spirits, calm the wind and the sea from its raging. The Apostle Peter watched as Jesus was transfigured.

At the trial, arrest and crucifixion of Jesus, the disciples—fearing for their own lives—denied knowing him, betrayed him, disassociated themselves from him and, eventually, Peter cursed His name.

How could they deny him after all they had witnessed and seen? They saw Him raise Lazarus from the dead. They walked with Jesus, talked with Jesus, broke bread with Jesus and listened to his wisdom, and yet they denied Him before men. WHY?

Jesus allowed the weaknesses of the disciples to be recorded in the Bible in order to teach all of us that in our humanity, no matter how much we KNOW about GOD, no matter how long we have sat in a church pew, we are just as capable as the disciples were to deny, betray, disassociate ourselves from God in spite of all the miracles we have seen around us in our lives. Under intense pressure, facing our favorite temptation, dealing with overwhelming stress, it is amazing what all of us have done and what we will do when we rely on our self-will and we think no one is watching. Secret abortions, quiet affairs, dishonest tax returns, over-inflated resumes, junk food binging, lying, drugs, DWI, shoplifting…and the list goes on and on and on.

When we get caught, the cry is the truth: "I'm only human." In our own humanity we fall so very short of what we really want to do. Why do we struggle so with the mind, the body and the soul?

There is a huge difference, my friends, between having the historical Jesus Christ around us, and having the Spirit Jesus Christ within us. The disciples, before being filled with the Spirit of Jesus, were weak, fearful, impotent and doubt-ridden; after being filled with the Spirit of Jesus, and after the day of Pentecost, they were different human beings. They became powerful, coura- geous, confident, faithful, kind and resilient. They spoke out about their faith with love, joy and peace. They healed the sick, they raised the dead, and they became Dunamis Leaders, endowed with a power that exceeded their own human strength. Dunamis can only be received after we have experienced, like the disciples, the failure of the self-willed life. Human failure fol- lowed by true humility is the first step toward receiving Dunamis.

* * *

Dunamis is an ancient Greek word for "Divine ability, might and power received and unleashed through the human spirit for the purpose of serving humanity with such awesome love, joy and peace that it glorifies God." As the Apostle Paul wrote in II Corinthians 4:7, "We have this treasure in fragile clay vessels, that the excellency of the power (Dunamis) may be of God and not of us." When people see our ordinary lives and see our extraordinary power to do good with such a powerful effect, it points to our divine Father in the universe.

Dunamis is the manifestation of divine power in created beings to lead and to serve others with love, joy, peace, patience, kindness, goodness, faithfulness, humility and self-control. These nine attributes are called the fruit of the Spirit, the evidence that a person is truly filled with Dunamis. The evidence is not in as to how well we can argue a religious point, or how well we can point out the faults in others, but Dunamis reveals how well we love our enemies, serve with joy, lead with humility and work for peace.

Galatians 5:22 describes these nine attributes as the "fruit of the Holy Spirit," not the fruits. The only fruit is love that is manifested in eight other characteristics. The word "fruit" really means "offspring," as the Bible states about the Virgin Mary's baby: "Blessed is ***the fruit*** of your womb, Jesus". So the fruit is the result of a coupling between God's Holy Spirit and our submissive humanity, which produces a new life in the womb of man's spirit, called *Agape* love. We birth a new life filled with Dunamis.

In Summary, when we confess to God that we are sinners, that in our own humanity we cannot please or begin to approach the holiness of God and when we accept the death of Jesus Christ as payment for our sins, we are at that moment filled with the Holy Spirit of Jesus Christ. This is what Jesus meant when he told his disciples, "I have to go so another can be sent, the

Comforter." In essence, He was telling them, "For three years I have been living with you, now I am going to live within you so I can continue my Father's work through my new body, called the Church: the universal body of my followers."

The Holy Spirit plants a seed called salvation into our spirit. That seed germinates and begins to take root as we water it with the Word of God, Fertilize it with Godly Fellowship and Cultivate it with Faith and Obedience. The seed begins to grow in our Spirit, getting stronger day by day, as we surrender our will to the will of the Holy Spirit. As we dig up the weeds of self-centeredness and cast them out, this allows for faster and deeper growth of the new life within us.

Just like a mother has to be careful what she eats when she is pregnant—everything she drinks, smokes and eats has a direct impact on the development of the new life growing in her womb—so we have to feed our spirits the pure milk of the word that gives health to our new life. As the seed grows, it cracks through the human spirit and starts to affect our human soul. The soul is the seat of our personality, our attitudes, our values, our inner thoughts. It is the part of us that makes us who we are. The Holy Spirit begins to change our soul. The soul then affects our actions, our decisions, our habits, our leadership style; we become a new creation with a new power that attracts the voluntary commitment of people.

Residing in humankind are two DNA strands. One strand is of natural parents, and one strand is of the Heavenly Father. Whichever one we feed, nurture and surrender to will dominate our personality, behavior, actions and decisions. That's why Jesus said, "No man can serve two masters: he will either hate the one or love the other." As Joshua said, "Chose you this day whom you will serve, for me and my house we chose to serve the Lord."

* * *

Dunamis is the spiritual dimension of the leadership dynamic.

Dr. Martin Luther King, Jr. received and unleashed Dunamis to challenge the soul of a nation to fulfill the promise of all persons being created equal and being endowed by their Creator with certain inalienable rights of life, liberty and the pursuit of happiness.

Dr. Martin Luther King, Jr. , as a college student, did not dream of becoming a Civil Rights leader. He attended Crozier Seminary in Atlanta and went on to pursue a Ph.D. in Philosophy. His nickname was "Tweed", because he always wore tweed suit jackets. He loved his life and wanted to pursue a career as a college professor to research, study and teach different philosophies. From Socrates to Hegel, Dr. King understood that the unexamined life is not worth living.

Foreshadowed by his own personal dreams, he died to live out the destiny that he was born to fulfill. As Paul wrote, "To live is Christ, to die is gain." The power that was unleashed through his life has yet to be seen again in the African American Community. As Dwight L. Moody, Founder of the Moody Bible Institute in Chicago, said: "The world has yet to see what God can do with one Man who totally committed to His Will, and I want to be that man."

* * *

Dr. King used the story of the Good Samaritan in his book,

Strength to Love, to explain why he left his personal agenda to follow a path of Dunamis. He explains that in the first century A.D. there was no such thing as a "good" Samaritan to the Jews. The Samarites and Jews were not fond of each other. It would be like saying today that Yassar Arafat is a "Good Terrorist". A "Good Samratian" was an oxymoron that would challenge a Jewish listener to really see where Jesus was going with this strange story.

Dr. King tells the familiar story of a traveler who is attacked, robbed and left for dead, and how three of his fellow countrymen travel by and see the man on the ground battered and bruised yet do nothing to help him. A Samaritan rides by and sees the man and stops, cares for the man, takes him to an inn and pays for his medical expenses. Jesus asks the question, "Who was this man's neighbor?"

Dr. King explained that the first three men who refused to stop to help their countryman thought to themselves, "If I stop to help this man what is going to happen to me, my schedule, my money and my reputation." Yet the Samaritan man asked, "If I don't stop to help this man, what is going to happen to him?"

Dr. King related the story to his own decision to serve a poor, black, angry people who would, by the end of his life in 1968, call him an Uncle Tom, Irrelevant, Antiquated and passé. Yet he served in saying, like Jesus, "Father forgive them for they know not what they do." Jesus said it best in the Garden of Gethsemane, "Not by my will but by thy will be done." How many of us are willing to die so that the spirit of God can be fully expressed through our lives? The impact we can have will last beyond our years on this planet.

Jesus lived only 33 years, never wrote a book, never traveled far beyond where he grew up, didn't have property, didn't have a political position, and didn't even own a grave for his own body after his death. Yet his name has torn the calendar into two, and, as Napoleon said, He is the most powerful figure the world has ever known.

* * *

Mother Teresa received and unleashed Dunamis to love and care for the unwanted, the rejected, the sick and the poor with a deep compassion and tenderness that has created an entire community of Nuns who do the work of God without fanfare or publicity. They clothe the naked, they feed the hungry and they visit and care for the least of these in Calcutta, India.

Dunamis has five components:

First, Dunamis is strength, ability and influence; an inherent power residing in a thing by virtue of its nature, or that which a person or thing puts forth. The power of the Spirit of Jesus Christ provides you and me with strength and ability to get things done. The power resides in the Spirit of Jesus and Jesus resides in you, therefore the Dunamis resides in you. As Jesus said, "Greater is he that is in you than he that is in the world. In this world you shall have tribulation, but be of good cheer for I have overcome the world."

In Chapter One I outline your Dunamis RQ, or your Resiliency Quotient, and how Dunamis helps you to overcome adversity, failure and setbacks. We then, who have the Spirit of Jesus Christ, are never without strength if we walk in the power of the Holy Spirit. We have that extra energy when the load seems too heavy to bear and makes it possible for us to carry the load the extra mile. The power of the Holy Spirit isn't always the power that pulls us out of situations; it is often the power that pulls us through them.

Secondly, Dunamis means "the power of working miracles." In chapters five, six and seven there are examples of real people who share their miraculous Dunamis experiences. Being delivered from drug abuse is a miracle; being delivered from sexual addictions is a miracle; being delivered from an abusive relationship can be a miracle. In Chapter Four I share the miracle healing of my youngest son, who was paralyzed from the chest down after a severe football injury.

Thirdly, Dunamis means moral power and excellence of soul. I write about your CQ, or Character Quotient, and how Dunamis received and unleashed affects your character, values, morals and attitudes. As we all know, what is done in the dark eventually comes to light—and at the worst possible time. Just ask Bill Clinton about blue dresses and Nixon about tape recorders.

Fourth, Dunamis means the power and influence that produces prosperity and success. Jesus said, "Seek you first the Kingdom of God and His righteousness and all these things will be added unto you." Joshua said, "This book of the law shall not pass out of your mouth, but you will mediate on it both day and night; then you will make your way prosperous and you will have good success." Dunamis will help you see opportunities that you have never seen before and lead you to situations that will be a blessing to you.

Fifth, Dunamis means delegated power. As a Dunamis leader you have been empowered with a power that makes you an ambassador of the kingdom of the most high. Jesus has given you power of attorney to act on His behalf with love, joy, peace, patience, kindness, goodness, faithfulness, humility and self-control. If you are acting in His service and not your own you will act with a power that will astonish you.

* * *

Now that you know what Dunamis is, let's begin to understand how to fully unleash it—to change the world one soul at a time.

The religious leaders of Jesus' time plotted to kill him because he offered a new paradigm of love, joy and peace—an intimate relationship with the Creator of the universe. The religious leaders were threatened by this new voice, which they believed would overturn their hold on the minds and hearts of the people. These men of God and faith decided that this Jesus had to be "downsized" and "relocated." Trusting followers were left in the ashes of confusion and bewilderment. That's where the twelve were after the death of their leader. They didn't think that life was worth living.

The life and ministry of Jesus teaches us that failure is the most important part of success. Failure need never be final. Failure is not in **falling** down, but in **staying** down. Jesus has taught us, by example, that when life knocks us down, we must land on our backs—because if we can look up, then we can get up; so we should never, ever give up. Knocked down, but never knocked out!

Some of our greatest inventors, politicians, business professionals, artists, authors and religious figures had to endure tremendous failure before they experienced success. Quite often in life, before you have a breakthrough, you will almost have a breakdown. All of the new births come from chaos, pain and confusion. A newspaper editor fired Walt Disney because he lacked creativity. Disney went bankrupt several times before creating the "Mouse that Roared." Thomas Edison's teachers said he was too stupid to ever learn. Albert Einstein did not speak until he was four years old, and did not read until he was seven. His teachers described him as mentally slow, unsociable and adrift forever in a world of foolish dreams. He was expelled and was refused admittance to Zurich Polytechnic School. He worked in anonymity for years as an office clerk, before his genius was expressed. The father of the famous sculptor, Rodin, said, "I have an idiot for a son." Described as the worst pupil in the school, Rodin failed three times to secure admittance to the school of art. His uncle called him "a waste of good sperm." Henry Ford failed and went broke FIVE TIMES before he finally found success with the Ford Motor Company. Winston Churchill failed the sixth grade. His life was full of defeats and setbacks. But then, at the age of 62, he became the Prime Minister of England. Indeed, his greatest contributions came in the twilight of his years. Even Colonel Sanders was 65 and bankrupt before he began building his KFC Empire. Bankers refused him funding 1099 times before he convinced someone to finally say, "yes."

Consider the resume of Abraham Lincoln — the ultimate "successful failure":

1831:	*Started his first business—**went bankrupt***
1832:	*Ran for State Legislature—**lost***
1832:	*Applied for Law School—**rejected***
1833:	*Began second business on borrowed money—**bankrupt again***

1835:	*Engaged to be married—****fiancée dies***
1836:	*Suffered a nervous breakdown—****bed-ridden for*** ***six*** **months.**
1836:	*Sought to be Speaker of the House—****defeated***
1840:	*Sought to become an elector—****defeated***
1843:	*Ran for Congress—****lost***
1846:	*Ran for Congress again—****won***
1848:	*Ran for re-election to Congress—****lost***
1854:	*Ran for the U.S. Senate—****lost***
1856:	*Sought the Vice Presidency—****lost***
1858:	*Ran for the Senate again—****lost***

Yet, despite a long record of failure, Abraham Lincoln was elected President of the United States of America in1860. He saved the Union, freed the Slaves and became one of the most beloved and respected leaders in world history.

Now let's look at another leader who failed miserably before he received and unleashed Dunamis on a lanai in Maui a few years ago. He became a Senior Pastor at the age of twenty-three. But after three years the church had had enough of his arrogance and egomania, so he resigned. His first wife, sick of his control-ling, arrogant and prideful behavior, left and divorced him — taking with her their two young children.

He became a corporate executive, Director of Organizational and Leadership Development for a Fortune 500 Corporation. He treated people like disposable razors—either they stayed sharp or he freed up their future. He was cold, detached, distant and controlling.

At age 26, after his divorce, he was living in a run-down, dirty apartment with a mattress on the floor. In this dirty, run-down place, the young man hit rock bottom and began to build, brick by small brick, what would become a leadership-consulting firm that would help leaders who needed renewal and retooling. The lessons he learned from his own failures, as they related to the dangers of pride, arrogance, temptation, power, ego and blind ambition, he would now use to coach and inspire leaders, managers, clergymen, politicians and athletic coaches around the world. He would become one of the most sought-after speakers and leadership consultants in the corporate community. Firms pay him up to $20,000 per hour to share his insights on Dunamis Leadership. His themes:

- Failure is never final: it is not the falling down, it is the staying down.
- Strategy: Remain humble, Pray, Seek God's Face and Turn from Evil.
- Vision: Whom God uses greatly, He wounds very deeply.

Today, at age 38, he is an author, he has remarried and has four children, lives in both Ohio and Maui, he is host of a national television program and was invited to join Tom Peters, Stephen Covey and Ken Blanchard 's "Lessons in Leadership Consortium," a leadership think tank for world leaders. He and his wife are in the midst of expanding their ministry and leadership institute in Maui, Hawaii, to continue his work with burned-out leaders who have lost their way. Out of his misery he found his mission. His name is Ronaldo I. Archer: the author of this book.

If you can look up, then you can get up—so never give up

After the death of Jesus, His twelve followers went fishing to take their minds off of their sorrow. While on the boat, failing to catch even a cold, a man on the shore called to them: "Children, have you any meat?" (In essence, "Have you caught anything?") Having failed as disciples, they were now are failing in the one thing they knew how to do well. They yelled back to the stranger on the shore, "We haven't caught a thing." They could have lied to spare their egos and pride. They could have said, "Oh Yea! And we are about to get a big load." Instead, they admitted they were failing yet again. The man on the shore told them to throw their nets on the other side of their boat. What a profound and curious command! How could he – who was standing on the shore — know where the fish were? It took great effort to bring the heavy, wet slippery net into the boat, recoil it and then to fling it over the other side. It also took great faith. After all, the man on the shore was asking the twelve to completely change direction and try something totally different.

How willing are we to do the same?

We have all heard the old saying, "If you keep doing what you've been doing, you will keep getting what you have been getting." Yet, we often resist positive change. Let's face the truth: it is hard to change our lifelong habits, traditions, customs, behaviors and mindsets.

We have all ridden in a car with a driver who is lost, but who will not admit it or who will not stop to ask for directions. His pride and stubbornness keeps him driving in a direction that is taking him further and further away from the true destination.

If you try to hint that he needs to admit that he is lost and needs to turn around, he might kick you out of the car. Soon, what started out to be a fun family trip turns into the Simpsons and the Griswolds meet in the Mutiny on The Bounty. In many cases it is not until the driver is hopelessly lost and has wasted time, gas, and money and everyone's patience that he will finally admit he took a wrong turn 65 miles ago. To stave off a coup, he will finally relent and turn the car around, finally going in the opposite direction.

Transcendent Leadership requires a ruthless self-examination. It requires a humble admission that you have lost your way. Somewhere along the line you took a wrong turn and for the past 5 years – perhaps longer – you have resisted every chance to admit it.

The disciples listened to the stranger and changed their methods, immediately hitting a mother lode of fish. In fact, they caught so many fish that their nets began to tear. Jesus is asking us today to throw our nets on the other side of our boat: to change our methods, our schemes and our strategies.

Are you tired of fishing and not catching anything? Is what you are doing working? If you can give up those old habits and actions that have always led to "bad success" ("bad success" is a plan that starts out looking good, but always ends in disappointment), then I am here to tell you that all of you can have it all. By "all," I mean love, joy, peace and a prosperous life—which are by-products of Dunamis.

Since September 11th, many people are rethinking their lives, ambitions, vocations and priorities. A fact of life is that trouble is with you now—either just leaving or on its way. Life is a volatile mixture of the unexpected, wrapped up in the mystery of the unexplained, blended with the shock of its eventual finality. Life does not promise success, happiness, health and wealth, but it does guarantee aging, illness and death – for us and for those we love.

For example, medical experts have concluded that no matter how healthily a man lives, he will eventually contract prostate cancer if he lives long enough. Our DNA contains weaknesses from our family lineage that will eventually do us in.

Some may call this the result of the "Sin" virus downloaded from forefather Adam when he disobeyed God in the Garden of Eden. His blood became contaminated with the Sin virus and now everyone is born with that death gene in his DNA.

We humans can do a lot of things. We can grow corn in the desert, transplant a pig's heart into a human host, split the atom, and create computers with artificial intelligence. We can do all of this, but we can't stop hate, violence, murder, rape, drug abuse, school shootings, war and death. What is it about the human creature that makes it so we can subdue everything around us, but we can't subdue the monsters within?

The Apostle Paul said in the Book of Romans, "When I try to do good, evil is right next to me. The good I want to do, I don't. The evil I do not want to do, I do. Oh wretched man that I am, who will save me from this misery?"

* * *

Isn't it amazing that we don't have to teach children how to lie? It is intuitive. You might ask a child, whom you saw take a candy cane off the Christmas tree, "Who ate the candy cane off the tree?" and the child might blurt out, "It was the Grinch."

What is sin? Sin is not so much an act, as it is a state of

being. Christians believe that humankind was born into sin because of the original sin of Adam. The sinful nature of humankind has long been demonstrated for all to see. Through the years, humankind has seen the Crusades, the Inquisition, the Transatlantic slave trade, the Holocaust, and the genocide of the native Hawaiian and Native American populations. Even today, we live with Black-on-Black crime in our inner cities, slavery still being practiced today by Africans against other Africans, domestic violence, pornography, prostitution and all forms of child abuse. What is the cure for the horrid state of humankind? From a Christian perspective, it is a legal issue. Let me make my make my case with this analogy:

A very strict judge, who is known for throwing the book at convicted criminals, is on the bench presiding over an infamous murder case. The defendant is accused of crimes against humanity, and the law of the jurisdiction requires the death penalty for these crimes. The man is tried and found guilty. The judge is ready to pronounce the sentence of death, when he looks over the bench and realizes for the first time that the convicted criminal is his own son. His son has had plastic surgery and looks nothing like the person the judge once knew; but as he looks into the convicted man's eyes, the judge realizes this is indeed his son, who had run away from home ten years ago.

The judge is faced with a somber dilemma: as a father he wants to show mercy to his long-lost son and spare him the death sentence, but as a judge it is his obligation to uphold the law. He is torn between his heart and his duty.

This is the exact same situation God found Himself in with Adam in the Garden of Eden. Adam broke a law of obedience and faced the death penalty. Just like the judge, God was obligated to uphold the law, but was dismayed because of His love for His creation and He wanted to show mercy. What was God to do?

Let me take you back to the courtroom. After much deliberation, the judge is prepared to announce the sentence of death upon his own son. Tears flow down his cheeks as he prepares to pound the gavel to pronounce judgment. Suddenly, before the judge makes his pronouncement, a man in the courtroom stands and says, "Your Honor, stop! Don't sentence this man to death. I am this man's best friend and because I love you both so much I am willing to take the punishment for his crime. I understand that the law must be satisfied and someone has to die for the crime. Kill me so that the law can be preserved and so you can also show your son mercy and grace."

That is what Jesus Christ did for us, my friends. He took the penalty of sin onto himself and died to fulfill the requirements of the law, which was death. He died so that God could show forth His grace and mercy to all who accept the innocent, sacrificial death of Jesus Christ in exchange for the gift of life.

That is what John 3:16 is all about when it says: "For God so loved the world that He gave His only begotten son, that whosoever believeth in Him should not perish, but have everlasting life." Death is not just physical, but is a permanent separation from our eternal Father.

My friends, while we were yet sinners, Christ died for us so that we could receive a life full of a new power, a new strength, a new courage, and a new boldness called DUNAMIS. When you accept Jesus' death as atonement for your sins and believe in your heart that God has raised Him from the dead, He then gives you access to His Holy Spirit, that will empower you with the same power Jesus had on the earth.

Successful navigation of life is our response to pain, wounds and failure. When life happens to you, it will either make you better or bitter. While I can't control life, I can control my response to it. There is a force available to you that makes it possible to conquer life's challenges. It is the same force that turned the twelve disciples from a bunch of confused and frightened fishermen, into world leaders and powerful healers of wounded souls. It is called DUNAMIS, Transcendent Power.

I think nature does the best job of demonstrating how pain is necessary for power and wounds are necessary for wisdom. One of the most interesting creatures in the ocean is the oyster. The oyster is not a very attractive-looking creature. Its shell is really quite homely when you compare it to the outward beauty of its cousin the clam—whose shell is so pretty that people collect them. The beauty of the oyster is hidden; it is deep within and will only be produced through pain. When a grain of sand finds its way inside the oyster's shell and lodges itself against the oyster's soft underbelly, it will, over time, become an irritant. As time progresses, the debris begins to cut a deep scar into the oyster's tissue. When the wound is deep enough and the pain is searing enough, the creature releases an enzyme to heal the deep wound. The enzyme hardens, and still more is secreted: layer after layer is laid over the grain of sand until a pearl is produced.

My friends, it is only when we have come to the end of ourselves and realize that our own strength is not enough to overcome life's challenges, that we open ourselves to receive the gift of Dunamis. It is only when our wounds are deep enough, our pain searing enough, that we cry out in humility to the Almighty. It is only then that the power of Dunamis is released through God's

Holy Spirit.

That's why Jesus said in his Sermon on the Mount, "Blessed are the poor in spirit, for they shall see the kingdom of God. Blessed are those who mourn, for they will be comforted." We are poor in spirit when we recognize that something is missing in our inner being.

The greatest journey is the journey inward. Once you start to probe your own wounded soul, you begin to weep and mourn. You confront those forces that keep you from experiencing Dunamis: your pride, your ego and your unwillingness to admit your need for unconditional love and acceptance. After all, aren't all of us searching for unconditional love and acceptance?

We try to get love and acceptance through our accomplishments, through titles, through wealth, through sex, through fame, through physical perfection, through mental expansion. We can obtain all these things. We can "have it all," so to speak, and find in the end that our souls are still crying for something that all these accomplishments just didn't heal. As Henry David Thoreau said, "most men lead lives of quiet desperation."

A speaker I once heard said about life, "I don't tell you who I am because you may not like me and that is all that I have." If we are not careful, we can live our lives with the phony veneer that our marriages are perfect, our kids are flawless and that we are the captains of our souls, wanting for nothing.

Then life happens to you, as it does to all of us.

All of us go through something, to something, to become something, and Dunamis can only fill that which has been emptied out. As long as you convince yourself that **you** are in charge and **you** are in control and you **can** handle it all, you will never receive and be able to lead with the power of Dunamis.

Because people today are hurting and have been wounded deeply by September 11th, they need leaders who are in touch with their own humanity and can project real feelings of love, compassion and empathy. We cannot teach what we do not know, and we cannot lead where we are not willing to go. We can't give what we don't ourselves possess. People need more than position power as they face complexity, competition and change.

When New York City and our nation were shaken to their cores by the terrorist attacks, we cried out for a leader who was filled with the power of Dunamis. We found one in the Mayor of New York City: Rudy Giuliani.

One year before September 11th, Rudy Giuliani was preparing to run for the U.S. Senate against Hillary Clinton. The polls showed him with a solid lead against the former First Lady. Then, out of the blue, he announced that he had contracted prostate cancer and was quitting the race. Later, he announced that his marriage was ending. I can't imagine anything more traumatic for a man than to have to deal with prostate cancer and its complications —including its effects on one's sex life and libido. The trials seemed to transform the tough former prosecutor who finally locked up John Gotti, the Dapper Don. The get-tough Mayor of New York was different now, as he spoke of how the challenges he faced changed him.

He committed to spend his final year in office reaching out to the hurting, the wounded and the forgotten. Suddenly, the crusty, tough-as-flint mayor sounded more like Mother Teresa than the tough former prosecutor who brought down the mob. Who would have known that God was preparing this man through his own pain and illness for the great challenge that awaited all of us on a clear September morning? Who could have imagined how magnificently he would bear the pain of millions? Indeed, Giuliani was so effective during that dark time in our nation's history that he drew comparisons with Winston Churchill, whose own leadership was so crucial to the eventual victory of the Allies during World War II. We all recall how Giuliani seemed to be everywhere at once, reaching out from his own wounded soul to the people of his city and his nation with a healing power of love and compassion. What we witnessed in Mayor Giuliani was unleashed Dunamis. Leadership so galvanizing that Time Magazine chose him as their "Person of the Year."

What Rudy Giuliani did was tap into a supernatural presence that gave him an unwavering confidence in the future, spiritual resiliency and an inner calm in the midst of chaos and confusion. That is why he attracted the voluntary commitment of so many others. When you unleash Dunamis, people won't say "I **have** to follow you," they will say, "I **get** to follow you!"

Chapter 3

Do You Have Dunamis?

The ancient Greeks so loved the concept of power that they used two words to define it. The first word used for power in the Greek is *Exousia*, which is the kind of power one earns based upon one's station in life, or position within an organization. This is where we get our English word "executive;" it is authority based solely on title. In the lexicon of organizational development it is called "position power": your title of manager, captain, president, mother or coach grants you a level of respect and reverence. But, if you study the teachings of leadership experts like Peter Drucker, John Maxwell and Ken Blanchard, it is clear that titles, degrees, status and position alone are highly overrated. Soldiers will always salute the rank, but they will only follow the person. *Exousia* leaders can be competent, organized, administrative managers that use the "command and control" method of management. They rely heavily on the status of their offices to get things done. They might communicate through impersonal means, remaining cold, distant, and aloof. Or, they might be very personable, affable, and warm—similar to the coach who slaps folks on the back and uses all the motivational tricks in the book: quoting Churchill, King, and Kennedy, telling great stories and jokes, cajoling people, relying on his easy-going, relaxed style to accomplish goals. Sometimes such leaders get taken advantage of because many mistake their kindness for weakness. The would-be usurpers then try to take over the group—hoping that the romper room leader doesn't have the spine to stand up and demand respect and results.

In the end, both of these *Exousia* leader-types are burned out, tired and end up failing to have the long-term impact they had hoped for. Sadly, they fall victim to the law of diminishing returns. No matter how gifted, intelligent, wise and skillful *Exousia* leaders are, they cannot sustain the momentum needed to create the legacy they so desire. They create organizations and work groups that look good, while going nowhere.

They have earned grudging compliance, but not whole-hearted commitment. Eventually, the amount of personal energy they have to expel takes a tremendous toll on their health, their families and their souls. They are successful, but the price they have paid for success has been steep. It is not about our leadership style. As long as we think it is our good looks, our mental brilliance, our charismatic flair—we will never experience true transcendent power. Position Power today is simply not enough. It is about the source of power, the source of strength, and the source of influence.

Blight Christmas

A father was raising his son, using put-downs and harsh words as a means to motivate him. He never once hugged his son or told him that he loved him. The father had a very successful, but all-consuming occupation. Though he was at the top of his profession, he turned to the bottle to deal with the stress of maintaining his success. His drinking would intensify the mistreatment of his son. It seemed that the father was at his worst during the Christmas season. Every Christmas, he would get drunk and ruin the holiday for the entire family. He would curse and beat his son quite regularly. One day, the son had enough and told his father that he hated him and someday he would get even with him. As the years went by, the son grew up into a drug-using, despondent young man who hated the Christmas holiday season because his memories of Christmas were always sad and painful. He expressed an extreme dislike for the Christmas movies television networks broadcast over and over again during the holiday season, movies that portrayed loving families hugging one another, exchanging gifts and kissing under the mistletoe. *White Christmas* was the movie he particularly loathed because he wanted a father like the warm, loving father characterized in the film.

One Christmas Day, as he watched an episode of *White Christmas*, he decided to get even with his mean and abusive Dad; and on that tragic day the son of Bing Crosby put a gun to his head and took his own life. He finally got even with his father. The world would know what a hypocrite Bing Crosby was once his suicide note became public.

Bing Crosby, who had earned the title of "America's Father" for his performance in *White Christmas*, lost his own son due to his failure to build a healthy and loving fatherly relationship with him. Bing had the position power that came with the title of father, but not the "Dunamis Power." He held a high position, but where it really counted he was Missing in Action.

Success without Dunamis requires a very high price. How long will you continue to make the payments on a career that it is bankrupting you and your soul? How long will you look good, while your life goes nowhere? How long will you continue to drive in the wrong direction, even though the sign ahead flashes that the bridge is out?

You can either carry buckets of water
or let a river of flowing water carry you.

There are two ways to bring water to a parched, arid community. If the water supply is 35 miles uphill from the village, you can either get buckets and go fetch the water, or you can dig up and empty out some earth to create an irrigation canal that will allow the life-giving water to flow through the emptied space.

Which would you rather do? Carry buckets of water or dig an irrigation system? *Exousia* is carrying buckets of water, while Dunamis is allowing a stream to flow through you. The difficult part about Dunamis is that you have to empty yourself of your **SELF** (ego, pride, self-will, etc...) in order to allow the supernatural power to flow through your leadership, your communication, your plans and your dreams. Dunamis is not revealed in the doing, but in the being. Then, from the being flows powerful and anointed doing.

When Moses met God face-to-face concerning the great task of leading the Hebrews out of Egyptian slavery to the promised land, he asked the Almighty: "Who shall I say has sent me?" The Almighty responded, "Tell them that I AM THAT I AM has sent you to free them from their bondage." He didn't tell

Moses: "I DO what I DO has sent you", but "I AM." WOW. We have lost this powerful concept in modern, Western society. God created us in His image to be human beings, not human doings. We confuse activity with accomplishment. We really want love and we think if we work hard enough, make enough money and do enough great things that people will love us. Quite the contrary; people will use you, people will flatter you and people will hang on to you as long as you are the mule pulling the wagon. But get sick, lose your job, lose all your money and see how many will help get back what they helped spend and party away. A very small, inner circle will be with you through the famine as well as the feast.

If you remember the story of Moses, he had tried earlier to free his people from bondage with his own strength by killing an Egyptian. The next morning, when the headlines hit the news-stands, instead of leading a revolution, Moses began a one-man, 100-mile dash out of Egypt to avoid getting killed.

Have you ever been run out of a leadership position because you tried to lead some great change effort and failed miserably? Moses had been so traumatized by his failure that when he was told it was time to go back and try again (but this time with Dunamis), he gave the Almighty every excuse in the book. Moses said, "Uh, you know they tried to kill me the last time I attempted this deliverance project and uh, you know that the trauma of it all gave me a speech impediment and a slight facial tic. Ever since the Egypt thing, I have developed a slight stutter, and just thinking about going back makes the stuttering worse. I, uh, think you need to send somebody who has a better track record, someone who has had success delivering people, perhaps someone with a Ph.D. in bondage-breaking. Because I failed so

miserably, my name is linked with Forest Gump. When the
ladies see me they yell, 'Run, Moses, Run!' and start laughing. I
think you better find somebody with some *Exousia.*"

But by now Moses was "Dunamis-ready" and we all know
what happened next. God does not need our abilities, but He
does need our availability: showing up can be more than half the
battle. Sometimes just showing up is enough. I know you may
not have the nicest clothes, I know you may not have any
money, no political connections, no family name. I know that
they have talked about you and rejected you and look at you
funny when you walk into the ballroom, but I DARE YOU TO
JUST SHOW UP. I received God's greatest blessings in my life
just by having the courage to show up. I felt out of place, my
one blue suit was shiny, had a hole in the inseam of pants near
my crotch because my fat legs wore a hole in the material by
rubbing together— but I showed up anyway and signed a million dollar contract.

David beat Goliath because he showed up; Abraham got
blessed with a son because he showed up; Joseph became second
in command of all of Egypt because he showed up. If you can
just show up, God will step up inside of you and part the Red
Sea, overcome the giant, find a ram in the bush and find food in
the midst of a famine. Joshua showed up and God showed out
and brought down the walls of Jericho. Dr. King showed up and
God showed out and changed the soul of America. Show up, so
God can show out.

The Journey to Dunamis

We are ready for the journey to Dunamis when and only

when we have tried every trick in the book and we have hit rock bottom; when we, like a bucking horse, have come to the end of our own strength and are ready to surrender our will to the will of God. What do you do when you have lost your way? The Almighty had to remind Moses that it wasn't about the *doing*, but the *being*—and the power of the doing always comes from the power of the being. This is why we are called human *beings* and not human *doings*.

We humans, especially we Westerners, are so busy trying to prove ourselves, to make a name for ourselves, that we run ahead of the power source needed to create lasting and meaningful change. While most target shooters practice with the method of "Ready! Aim! Fire!" *Human doings* tend to use "Ready! Fire! Aim!" Then, they spray, pray and hope to hit something – anything! Worse yet, some of us who, like Moses, after getting gangster-slapped around by life with the "Ready! Fire! Aim!" Method, become so traumatized that we use the "Ready, AIMM-MMMMMMMMMMMMMMMMMMMM! and never Fire!" Method.

Dunamis is not permanent. It lasts as long as you allow the Spirit to control your mind, body and soul. In a sense, Dunamis works like alcohol. Simply reading the label on a bottle of Jack Daniels is not going to get one drunk. Neither will pouring the contents on the ground get one drunk. It is only when the contents of the bottle are ingested that one is affected. The more alcohol is consumed, the more one's speech pattern, vision, hearing, sense of smell, motor skills, appetite and sex drive changes. However, if a person wakes up the next morning and doesn't ingest any more alcohol, their speech pattern, vision, motors skills and appetites return to "normal." It takes a daily consumption of the alcohol to create the effect of intoxication.

All of the above applies to the filling of your soul with the Spirit of God, which leads to Dunamis. Simply holding the Bible in my hand, simply holding prayers in my head, simply knowing what I am supposed to do is not going to get you drunk with Dunamis. You need to ask God each and every day to fill you with His supernatural presence.

In order to do this you must be aware of what you allow into your own spirit. What kinds of videos do you watch? What Internet sites do you visit? What do you listen to on the radio while you are driving? What kinds of television shows do you view? You are what you read, watch, hear and eat. Your spirit needs to be fed, just like your body and mind. Are you starving your spirit?

I went through this sort of spiritual malnutrition. I was so busy being busy, I began to starve my spirit. Day-by-day and week-by-week my spirit got weaker and weaker. One of the things my football coach used to say was: "Don't read your press clippings because you may start to believe all the hype. You must continue to do what you have done—not to just get to the top, but to stay at the top." I forgot that lesson and began to think the reason for my great success was me: my talent, my hard work, my risk-taking, my programs, my book, my television show. I stopped praying, stopped studying the Bible and began to worship the gifts, not the giver of the gifts.

I call the ages of 28 through 36 my "Lost Years," where I slipped back into the mindset of a human doing and not a human being. I was nothing more than what I achieved. I carried my accomplishments on my back. When people would meet me on the streets and engage me in conversation, it was as though they were in the middle of a sales call or a high-powered marketing campaign about the latest success of Ron Archer. If I couldn't talk about how much money I was making, the new article written about me in the *Wall Street Journal*, or the latest country I had just visited, I had nothing to say. I was so insecure, so anxious to prove that I had become successful, that success became an obsession. I became a success addict.

A great man once said: "Success is getting what you want, but happiness is wanting what you get." By all standards I was a success, but something was seriously wrong. I looked over my kingdom and reflected what I had done to achieve my dreams: the hard work, the sacrifices, the travel, the meetings, the tough choices and the time spent to get it all done. I was living the American Dream, yet it seemed so empty.

As an American success story I lived by the words of my favorite singer, Frank Sinatra: "I did it my way." I was a self-made man, having pulled myself up by my own bootstraps. The problem was that in my journey to make a name for myself, I left my first love. I had neglected my spiritual relationship. Where was God in all of this success? I had no time for God. I was too busy building my empire. My favorite movie had changed from *The Ten Commandments to The Godfather Parts 1 and 2.* I had to take care of "the family"; I had to become the "Don." I had no time for prayer or study because I was busy doing real work.

I thought to myself, God should be grateful to have someone like me. I don't drink. I don't do drugs. I don't hang out in the streets. I am a pretty decent guy. Why am I so driven to make a name for myself? What is pushing me to become a millionaire? Why do I need outward success to justify my existence?

Then I came to the realization that the shame and embarrassment of being an illegitimate child was driving me to do all of these things. I had no father and no true last name. So, I decided that my last name would be "Success." People would be forced to respect me. I would be somebody. I would have a title and build a half million-dollar dream home. I would have a Rolex and drive a BMW Z3 Convertible Roadster. I would have a national TV program and make a million dollars a year. I thought: if I achieve all these things, I will wash away the stain of illegitimacy; I will be whole again and my mother will love and be proud of me. I will be the great one.

A surprising thing happened, though. I achieved all of these things, and all I became was tired, sad and angry. Money, fame, success had not filled the emptiness in my soul. I just had a bunch of junk that would rust and decay. No matter how much I made, it was never enough. If I made a million, then making two million would fix the problem. I was trapped in an endless cycle of becoming something else and needing more and more money, success and power. I just couldn't be still. I didn't feel worthy of love and acceptance unless I was conquering some monstrous giant or climbing a great wall.

On January 2, 2000, a change came over me when my wife and I were in Maui on our annual retreat. If you have ever been blessed to visit Maui, you know it is a place of peace and calm. It is a very slow-paced and beautiful place to rest, pray and reflect. The people are so friendly, giving and loving. The natural beauty is so awesome that material possessions are dwarfed in comparison. So the people in Maui are more focused on spiritual beauty, personal health and nature. It is truly paradise on earth. It is my second home and the place where I found myself by finding God again. I was pacing on the lanai of our condo in Maui, and as I looked over the landscape of golden sandy beaches below, deep blue water, clear blue skies, and majestic volcanic mountains, I was struck by how the outward beauty contrasted with the ugliness within me. I hated what I had become. I hated who I was. What happened to that sixteen-year old who loved God and wanted to share God's love with the world? Like the prodigal son, I left my first love to go out and make a name for myself; and the name I made for myself was "FOOL." I had become everything I hated. I had fallen so far away from God that I didn't think he would ever take me back. I was so ashamed, so tired and so lost. I took out my day planner and the Gideon Bible that was in the condo and sat down in a lawn chair and wrote one question:

"Lord, I have lost my way, how do I get back to you!!"

I finally admitted that the car I was driving was heading in the wrong direction— that I was wasting time, gas and money, and now I needed to know how to get back home.

I didn't want religion. I had had enough of that to last me forever. I wanted to renew my relationship with my Creator, the source of all life. I had gotten so far off track and done so much damage that I wondered whether I would find my way back, or if it was already too late for me and I had become a lost soul — a reprobate (one without hope). I had water, but I was still thirsty; I had food, but I was still hungry; I had shelter, but I was still cold; I had fame, but I was still alone; I had money, but I was still poor; I had power, but I had no lasting positive impact on the lives of people. I was spiritually bankrupt.

Jesus said: "If a man tries to find himself, he will lose himself. But if a man will lose himself in me, he will find himself."

What does that mean?

Jesus meant only where there is nothing can the true value of a thing be found. Put another way, emptiness has value. When you can get over the fear of losing everything, then you are free to become anything.

Take, for example, the cup. Its usefulness is found in its emptiness, for then it can serve its true purpose: containing the essence of life. So it is with us. When we reach the state of humility wherein we empty ourselves of ourselves, it is only then that God can pour his Holy Spirit into us and fill us with the power of Dunamis. Humility is the ability to admit that what we have been doing is not working. It is standing before a mighty and loving God and crying out, "I am lost. Please help me to get back to you and the true purpose of my life." It is only then that we can ask ourselves questions like, "Why am I here on this planet?" and "How can I best maximize my gifts and talents to serve humanity?" And once emptied of self-centeredness, narcissism, pride, ego and shame, we—like the cup – are empty and ready to be filled with overflowing Grace.

For the first time in many years, I was ready to let the light in on a life filled with darkness and shame. On the lanai that day in Maui, while reading the book of Ecclesiastes, written by a very wise and rich man named Solomon, I discerned the seven principles of the self-centered life:

1. Control will always slip out of our grasp
2. Relationships will always disappoint
3. Work will leave us frustrated

4. Pleasure and success are fleeting
5. Knowledge and power alone are never enough to satisfy our longing for love
6. Religion without a relationship with God usually leads to legalism, living by a list of "do's" and "don'ts"
7. Life ends in decay and death

My usual strategy for dealing with life's messes was to seek control over them. I would always try to gain power in the world in order to have an effective foundation to manage my existence.

Power, whether it is power of status, ability, career or position ought to make us feel more in control. But I learned it doesn't. Just as I can't tame the power in the hurricane, the tidal wave or the earthquake, I learned I couldn't tame life.

Michael Jordan's power, money and fame couldn't save his father from being murdered by two young thugs. Bill Cosby's power, money and fame couldn't save his son from an immigrant Russian criminal and the same fate. Charles Lindbergh's fame, money and power didn't save his baby from being kidnapped and killed.

So, human power does not bring control along with it; and when we're brought to this realization we can be very disappointed. We can even lose the spark and vitality we need to live a good life.

It is in the state of humility and emptiness that God can fill us with His Divine Presence—called the Holy Spirit—which is the source of Dunamis. Dunamis can only empower us when we, in our supposed strength, admit we are, in fact, impotent and powerless to conquer the Goliaths that plague us. We, then, gain a power that can move the mountains in our lives, calm the storms within teams, raise dead relationships back to life, heal the broken-hearted and provide vision to blind organizations.

In II Chronicles 7:14, God explains how a lost soul returns to Him:

"If my people, who are called by my name, will humble themselves, and pray, and seek My face, and turn from their wicked ways, then I will hear from heaven, will forgive their sin and will heal their land."

Since September 11th, Americans are in need of healing. There is broken-heartedness in the land, a loss of hope and vision by children who no longer feel safe in their own schools. We need leaders who are tapped into the authentic power of healing and inspiration that is Dunamis. That power only comes from being filled with God's Spirit of love, peace and joy.

Humble yourself under God's mighty hand and he will left you up!

* * *

Do you know what kind of power is available to you?

The power to call forth those things that are not as you thought they were, the power to rise above circumstances and problems with confidence and joy, the power to have peace in the midst of chaos and confusion, the power to connect with the hearts of others in such a way that they are motivated and inspired to reach new levels of excellence and the knowledge to discern that all the events of your life have meaning, value and purpose. The power to be able to turn pain into power, wounds into wisdom and scars into stars is what DUNAMIS is all about.

Take it from this onetime bed-wetting, stuttering, fat kid who tapped into Dunamis and has watched as it has taken his life to new heights of love, joy and peace. If God can do this for me, He can do it for you. What are you waiting for? If you really want to experience Dunamis, then ask God these five questions.

1 **God, I have lost my way. How do I get back to you?**
   Read **II Chronicles 7:13-14** for a week. Meditate on it and listen for God's whispered voice.

2 **God, I have done so much damage to others and to myself, is it too late for me to be of any use?**
   Read **Luke 15:11-32** for a week. Meditate on its meaning.

3 **God, how do I avoid bad success and create good success for my life?**
   Read **Joshua 1:8-9** for a week. Meditate on the message God is sending you.

4 **God, is it true that you love me unconditionally with all my faults and scars?**
   Read **Romans 8:28-39** for a month. Meditate on God's unconditional love for you.

5 **What does it mean to be saved from sin?**
   Read the following: **Romans 3:10, Romans 3:23, Romans 5:8, Romans 6:23 and Romans 10:9-13**.

The Nine Attributes of the Dunamis Leader

In the book of Galatians 5:22-23 in the New Testament, the Apostle Paul lists the nine attributes of being filled with the Holy Spirit, the attributes that prove one has Dunamis: "But the fruit of the Spirit is love, joy, peace, patience, kindness, goodness, faithfulness, humility and self-control." If you are a Dunamis Leader, people will be able to see these attributes that attract others like a magnet to your cause or vision.

Love: *You have a Passion for People; Passion for Results; Passion for Excellence; Passion for Winning the Right Way.*

Joy: *Contagious Enthusiasm, Contagious Excitement, Contagious Energy and Contagious Commitment in spite of circumstances; Spiritual buoyancy.*

Peace: *Poise, Polish and Presence under Pressure; Quiet Confidence in the midst of Chaos and Confusion; Reassuring Calm in the midst of a storm.*

Patience: *Visionary; Sees the Big Picture; Plans the work and works the Plan. Does not Panic when things go wrong; Works the problem, Looks for solutions; does not play the blame game; Never Punishes an honest mistake while people are learning.*

Kindness: *Encourager, Motivator, Makes others feel Important; Excellent Listener; Shows Empathy;*

Catches people doing things right;
Thoughtful.

Goodness: Strong Character; Good Judgment; Fiscally Responsible; Frugal; Honest; Tactful; Can-do Attitude.

Dependable; Credible; Delivers on Promises Made; Follows up words with actions; Consistent Performer.

Humility: Shares the credit for success; openly admits when a mistake has been made; Forgiving of others; Turns the "ME into the "WE"; Team Builder.

Self-Controlled: Manages temper and Anger well; Sacrifices for the betterment of the organization; Treats others with respect and dignity; Leads by Example; Tough; Demanding, but Fair.

What is love?

The fruit of the spirit is one of the aspects of Love. The ancient Greeks had four words to describe this force that all humans long to posses and relish: Eros, Phileo, Stergos and Agape.

Eros is what we today call "erotic" or "physical" love—the passion and the emotion exchanged between newlyweds on their honeymoon. It is a love that lives to be expressed through a deep longing and a deep need to be significant. Some medical doctors believe that some chemicals in dark chocolate and red wine have similar effects as that of *Eros*; it just makes you feel good and tingly all over. We call this kind of love the "can't helps." You just can't help yourself. You want to be around the person all the time, just to hold hands, exchange glances, giggle and have fun.

Eros is also a very immature and selfish kind of love. *Eros* says, "I love you because you make me feel good, you meet my needs, you look good, you do what I want you to do and you are easy to love." *Eros* offers a continuous emotional "high" while in the presence of the person that you are attracted to. *Eros* can also apply to the love you have for winning, for making money, for playing golf or anything that gives you that rush of pleasure and sense of well-being. *Eros* can best be described as a temporary ecstasy, a fleeting fantasy and a marvelous movement.

I can honestly say after many, many years of marriage that my wife and I still have the "can't helps" for each other. We still have hot passion for each other. When I am out of town, which is quite often, we talk on the phone like teenagers. We are best friends and we love being around each other all the time. We have serious Bible studies, debates and discussions every day, either by phone or in person. As the Bible says about Adam and Eve, they were naked and not ashamed. Completely transparent to each other; no hiding place, no games, just naked and not ashamed. How many get naked with someone and the next day you feel ashamed. Why do you feel ashamed? Are you hiding something? Are you compromising your true values to be with this person? Ask the question and search for the answer. The unexamined life is not a life at all.

* * *

Phileo is the love that the great city of *Philadelphia* is named after. *Phileo* means that we love those who look, act, think and behave like us. It is brotherly love, sisterly affection, belonging to the same fraternity, sorority, social club and religious group or sports league. It is a love for those who share similar passions with you—which, in turn, draws you together to achieve a common vision, goal or objective.

* * *

Stergos is the love that a mother has for a child—the highest form of human love. It is the kind of love that wants to nurture, support and care for another. *Stergos* feels obligated to safeguard and to defend the welfare of another. It is a love that feels responsible for the success and the development of another.

My oldest son, Cedric, is in college and sends me an email, "No 'mon', no fun your son." I replied, "So sad, too bad, your dad." Mothers usually do not respond like this. Instead, they tell the needy child to come on home and there will be something special in the folded, clean laundry: folded, clean money!

The best example of this kind of love, that I personally witnessed, was the love that my grandmother demonstrated to her children and grandchildren. My grandmother was a German-Hungarian woman who married an African American/Cuban man in the 1940's. Her parents disowned her for marrying out of her race and having seven bi-racial children. Her husband went to jail for a time for beating a man for calling his wife a "nigger lover". During his imprisonment, she had one of her eyes removed due to cancer. Her parents made her an offer. If she would give up her "nigger" children, she could come back to her middle class, white world. She refused the offer because of her strong commitment to her children.

I loved that woman. She was so special. She loved to cook and she would always whistle. Her favorite singer was Freddie Fender and the two songs of his she played all the time were, "Wasted Days and Wasted Nights" and "Before the Last Tear Drop Falls." The best times of my childhood were spent with her. I remember her smoking her Kool's Extra Long menthol cigarettes and sipping her coffee. At her funeral my uncle Donald summed her up best when he said, "She would give you her last dollar, the shirt off her back—but don't ever ask her for her last cigarette."

New Year's Eve's were great events for all the grandkids because of her. It would start with Happy, Buddy and Buster playing spades with Allen, David and Cindy. They would sit around a smoke-filled room and play cards for hours. It was a rite of passage when they invited you to sit at the table and dealt you in. Around nine o'clock all the grown ups would leave and the all grandkids would be gathered at "Granny's Rock'n Roll New Year's Eve Celebration." She would cook homemade pizza, homemade donuts, hamburgs and french fries. There would be April, Jody, Tony, TT, Antuan, Steven, Jamie, Junior, Ronnie, Shawn and Monster, all gathered at Granny's house for the weekend. Talk about some fun times! It was the best. It wasn't about money, a big house, or fancy furniture, because Granny did not have any of those things. She just had a lot of Dunamis. She made each grandchild feel special and important.

The big moment came at 12 o'clock midnight, and Granny would open the windows and with all our heads hanging out, we would yell "Out with the old and in with the new, Happy New

Year." Now, the funny thing was, the City of East Cleveland is one of the poorest cities in Ohio and at midnight people were shooting their guns and blasting their shotguns. We were lucky we didn't get our heads blown off!

Other than my grandmother, the family members that best demonstrate *Stergos* are my aunts Cindy and Lorraine. My Aunt Cindy is my guardian angel. She was always there for me when I needed help. I went to a Catholic high school and Aunt Cindy paid my tuition. When I went off to college, she made sure I always had money in my pocket. When I needed my first car, Cindy co-signed for a brown Volkswagen Rabbit. When I needed a job, she let me work for her and her husband's property management company as a painter. Whenever I got into trouble, she was always there to help me—no questions asked.

In my twenties, when I lost it all and lived in a one-room roach-infested apartment with a mattress on the floor, she was my first investor in the new business venture I was starting. For a whole year, she paid for all my travel expenses so I could fly around the country building my dream. If it were not for my guardian angel, Cynthia Paci Hughes, I would not be where I am today. Thanks, Cindy, for being the wind beneath my wings and supporting me during the most difficult times of my life. I love you.

Lorraine Paci Walters, another exhibitor of *Stergos*, is the best Christian I have ever met. When her brother, Buster, became ill and had some serious health problems, she moved him and his youngest daughter and grandson from Cleveland to Florida to live with her, and then went on to adopt his youngest daughter. This was after she put her own son, Jody, through college and graduate school. She was now single, child-free and ready to mingle. She put off her own agenda to help her brother in a time of illness. She has demonstrated selflessness and is a great woman of love and mercy. She is the person who is most like Granny. Today, Uncle Buster has fully recovered from his ill health and is doing great thanks to his loving sister, Lorraine. God Bless you for your love and sacrifice.

* * *

Agape is the kind of love that can only be shared through being filled with Dunamis. It loves those who are unlovable. It loves those you don't like. It loves in spite of, rather than because of. It is unconditional and uncompromising. *Agape* love is active. It demands expression. It is never passive. *Agape* seeks an object to serve and to sacrifice for. *Agape* is not good intentions: it is good action. *Agape* is under the control of the will to act in a manner that puts God's agenda first, others' needs second and ourselves last.

Everyone in society desires, to some extent, to be loved and to show love, yet many are not loved or are not capable of love. Love is a choice, a decision to make.

In summary, *Agape* is the will to extend one's self for the purpose of nurturing another's physical, intellectual and spiritual growth in spite of how we may feel. *Agape* is to follow the commandments of Jesus, who said: "Love the Lord your God with all your heart, mind and soul, and love your neighbor as yourself." It also means the ability to turn the other cheek and to seek the salvation of your enemies. Examples are: Dr. Martin Luther King, Jr. praying for the salvation of Bull Connor, Jimmy Carter leading a communist leader from the former Soviet Union to Christ and, finally, Jesus, at His crucifixion, saying from the cross, "Father, forgive them for they know not what they do." When we can love our enemies and pray for the salvation of those who personally persecute us, then we know we have reached the level of *Agape*. For *Agape* says, "I can love you because God has loved me."

Jesus said, "Love the Lord your God with all your heart, all your mind and all your soul. Love your neighbor as yourself." Love for God is exclusive, concentrated and all-consuming. It is seeking the face of God. It is seeking to know God with all of our being, to forgive those who have injured us, and to pray for those who wish to see us harmed. How do you know when you are full of Dunamis? When you can love, forgive and pray for that person whom, in your humanity, you love to hate.

Chapter 4

How Dunamis will enhance and improve your IQ, TQ and CQ

Leaders today must improve the speed, the quality and quantity of their information funnels. Managing in the Information Age, leaders are being viewed more and more as information conduits. Information must flow effortlessly from east to west and from north to south. Accurate, relevant and timely information is the lifeblood of any successful leader's management body.

Imagine how different our lives would be if the CIA would have known on September 10th what was being planned for September 11th—if they had access to accurate data that would have identified the who, what, when and where of the planned terrorist attacks.

But how do we get such accurate information to keep us razor-sharp and ever-ready for change? People have to trust us. People must believe in our integrity before they will share their innermost secrets, ideas, formulas and strategies with us. What was it about Bob Woodward, a best selling author and the **WASHINGTON POST** executive of Watergate fame, that made people in highly sensitive positions in the military, the corporate sector and the government spill their guts to him? He always seemed to know what was going on in the CIA, the Joint Chiefs of Staff and the scandal-plagued Clinton White House.

But why?

He has proven himself as a professional who knows how to protect the identity and confidentiality of a source. It has been over 25 years since the name "Deep Throat" entered the lexicon as the classic background insider who knows all, sees all and hears all. People are still trying to guess the identity of Deep Throat. But only God, Bob Woodward and Carl Bernstein know who it is—and they will never tell on or off the record.

We call this attribute of trust: leadership credibility. What is "leadership credibility?" It is impossible to increase your Information Quotient without it. Credibility is demonstrating good character, projecting good will and building arguments that make good sense.

Attributes of Good Character (Colin Powell)
1. Admits a mistake and takes responsibility for it
2. Looks for Win/Win solutions in relationship management
3. Has clearly defined moral boundaries in personal deportment
4. Looks to do the right thing for the right reasons
5. Is Consistent, Confident and Competent

Attributes of Good Will: (Oprah Winfrey)
1. Listens for understanding in others' points of view
2. Validates the opinions of others

3. Makes decisions that will benefit the whole
4. Makes others feel important and valued
5. Leads by example, serves others as a practice, not as a gimmick

Attributes of Good Sense: (Billy Graham)
1. Communicates to connect and inform, not to impress
2. Clear, Concise and Complete explanations
3. Short, Simple and Succinct agendas
4. Confronts with Humor
5. Humble, Self-Effacing and Relaxed manner

Information is the oil and the coal of the new millennium—a valuable commodity that causes the wheels of capitalism to revolve and progress. Whoever has the ability to increase their Information Quotient is going to dominate his or her market.

* * *

It was a Monday morning in the opulent, sleepless city of Las Vegas in late 1982, when computer "geeks" were converging on COMDEX, the largest computer trade show in America. Bill Gates was a young, 27 year-old computer up-and-comer who was attending the convention. As he walked along the enormous aisles of the trade show, he was struck by what he saw at VisiCorps' booth. What he saw would change him, his company, and the information technology industry forever. For when he looked at the computer screen, he expected to see the antiquated, cold DOS-based C:> prompt that his company, Microsoft, had standardized on all of IBM's PCs. Instead, he saw a revolutionary graphical interface called "VisiON." With the use of a mouse, users could execute a series of commands by pointing and click-ing on various icons. He was staring at a real paradigm shift in his industry that would make his software application, MS DOS, obsolete.

He had to get new information from the brightest minds in the industry. In order to do so, he hired Steve Wood from Yale to manage Microsoft's struggling Interface Manager group. He also brought in Scott McGregor, the then 26-year-old graphics guru from Xerox Corporation. McGregor would later say that one of the things that impressed him most was not Gate's money, title or position, but his seemingly insatiable quest for knowledge and information. McGregor found out that if he ever knew more that Gates on a particular topic, instead of being put off, Chairman Bill would go out cram and bone up on the subject matter until he became an expert. He would always know what his top people knew so that he could never be black-mailed by the threat of someone taking their intellectual capital to another enterprise.

In late 1982, not long after Gates ordered his troops to learn everything in the universe about VisiOn's new software application, he embarked on creating what would become Microsoft's most marketable product: its image and brand name. The key to Microsoft's success was to have a naming strategy for all of Microsoft's products and for the company to enforce the brand. So instead of "Word" as a word processor, it would be called "Microsoft Word". Multiplan, Microsoft's spreadsheet, would be called "Microsoft Excel."

Gates learned from his research that products and product versions would come and go, but the Microsoft brand name would live on. This is called "selling the invisible." He dropped out of Harvard so he could think, learn and sell at the speed of thought. The IQ leader was driven not to work harder than the competition, but to learn faster and work smarter than the competition.

Information Quotient Tips:
1) Develop an insatiable hunger for knowledge
2) Commit to being a life-long learner
3) Listen and seek out opposing views to broaden your perspective
4) Read at least one book a week
5) Seek to mentor and to be mentored
6) Practice humility, it attracts knowledgeable people to your inner circle
7) The fear of God is the beginning of true wisdom

Talent Quotient

A leader's Talent Quotient is his ability to adroitly perform two functions. The first is to identify his innate gifts, skills and abilities, properly aligning them with a vocation and a career that best fulfills his desire to serve humanity and to glorify God. The second function is to skillfully evaluate the needs of his team/organization so he can recruit and develop talented people to meet those needs. Always staff your weaknesses and sharpen your strengths.

For the high TQ leader, the core values are:
1) Perfect your strengths and staff your weaknesses
2) Volunteer to put your talent to use: talent must be seen

to be rewarded
3) Place yourself in challenging situations to test the limits of your talent
4) Align your team's talents with the organization's vision, mission and priorities
5) Your talent, when perfected, will make room for you at the very top
6) Use your talent to glorify God and He will, in turn, give more opportunities to use your talent on a grander scale

The high TQ leader understands that no talent is so limited that we should feel ashamed to share it with the world. No amount of talent is so poor that humanity does not need it. All talents are too precious to be wasted by not using them or by using them for meaningless purposes.

The prisons are filled with brilliant men and women who wasted their great talents on illegal and meaningless purposes. How many young drug dealers in prison have the talent to be successful entrepreneurs in the legitimate world? How many con men could be skillful marketing and sales professionals in the legitimate world?

Tell me, friends, how many times have you had a great idea, but you talked yourself out of it? In the parable of the talents, a master who was leaving for a journey entrusted his money to his servants to invest and develop in his absence. To one he gave five talents; to another two; and to a third he gave one. On his return from his journey he asked for a report on the use of the talents that he gave them to invest. Two of the servants multiplied their talents and they grew exponentially. The one who was fearful and afraid to risk any loss, took his talent and hid it.

The master, then, took his talent and gave it to the one who was the most industrious.

Perhaps God has given you a dream or a new idea that would serve humanity well and, due to your fear of failure, you never put your idea into practice. I assure you that you will, one day, watch a program about someone who took the idea and built a profitable and successful business out of it. You will sit there in your easy-chair becoming uneasy because you had the same idea five years ago, only you never developed it.

How many people are "woulda, coulda, shoulda's," spending their lives confusing activity with accomplishment. They are wanderers, giving excuse after excuse about why they can't go back to school or leave a job that is killing them. They go to their graves never having played their best music.

The richest place in the world is not Fort Knox, Buckingham Palace or the oil fields of Saudi Arabia, but the cemetery; millions of unused talents and undeveloped geniuses are buried in every one. Who knows if the cure for cancer is in a cemetery somewhere, along with the answer to the complexities of black holes in space, which might provide the knowledge we need to use wormhole time travel to distance galaxies?

When I first met my wife she was a cook for an elementary school. I was teaching a seminar she attended. She turned in a term paper on leadership. She had no formal education after high school, but her writing and thinking was at a graduate level. I asked after class why she never attended college. She responded that she had just started attending a local community college and wanted to become a teacher.

Twelve years later my wife has graduated with honors from Case Western Reserve University with a Masters in

Organizational Development and Analysis. She is the Chief
Executive Officer for our family of companies and is a gifted
leader. She had hidden talent that became developed talent. Do
what you can, with what you have, with where you are so you
can improve and grow from there. What is your talent? What is
your gift? You have a destiny. Your first job is to find God and
God will help you find your destiny. King Solomon said,
"Where there is no vision, the people soon perish." What is
your vision for your life? Here are a few questions to help you
unearth your heavenly gift:

1) **What was a high point in your life as it relates to
   school activities, clubs or work assignments?**
   (Photography club, school newspaper, art class, music
   lessons, pottery class, gymnastics, ice skating, home
   economics, fishing, coaching, teaching Sunday School,
   building a shed with Dad, etc…)

2) **What was your best subject in School?** (Math,
   Science, Art, English)

3) **What, for others, is work, but for you seems like fun
   and comes easy?** (Repairing cars, writing poetry,
   balancing checkbooks)

4) **What are your hobbies?** What are you passionate about?
   What gives life to your life? (Coaching, Little League
   Sports, singing in choir)

5) **If you had three wishes to create the perfect job what
   would they be?** (Autonomy, Creative freedom, flexible
   working hours)

After you complete the above questionnaire, the next step is
to find someone who is currently involved in the activity or the

work in which you have an interest and ask that person if they wouldn't mind having you around as an intern or volunteer. Learn everything you can about the work and study everything you can about the subject. Always do more than what you are being asked to do—for if you do more than what you are being asked to do, you will get more opportunity to do what you really want to do.

Start small. Work your dream part-time until you earn enough to go full time. Identify key stakeholders, individuals who care about you and your dream. Develop a board of advisors. Ask questions. Never be ashamed to ask for help. Whatever you do, do it for the glory of God, do it with passion and energy. Offer your customers exceptional service. Don't aim for satisfaction, instead aim to delight them, hence transforming your customers into raving fans who will brag about you and your service to their friends and family. Under-promise and over-deliver by providing value-added service. Make people feel important and special by projecting Dunamis (love, joy and kindness) to everyone you meet. Never just make a living, but instead always live your making. Become a master at what you are going to do. Become personally committed and not casually involved. Personal commitment and casual involvement are like ham and eggs; with ham and eggs, the chicken was casually involved and the pig was personally committed.

There are three things you must do to transform your talent into an industry:

    1) Develop a vision statement for your life and vocation
        a. Define a set of core values that will forever guide you

        b. Define for yourself what is the preferred future state

2) Develop a persistent attitude to pursue your dream with vigor and tenacity

        a. Winners never quit and Quitters never win

        b. Your attitude determines your altitude

3) Develop a resilient attitude toward life

        a. Never take rejection personally, learn and grow from it

        b. Failure is the most important part of success, so don't fear it

        c. Speak your dream everyday; words give life to your dreams

Talent is like money and time: you must invest it wisely, spend it prudently and share it for it to prosper and grow. In order to grow talent you must have the faith to use it, because what you do not use you will eventually lose.

Character Quotient

"With all the power that a president has, the most important thing to bear in mind is this: you must not give power to a man unless, above everything else, he has character. Character is the most important qualification the president of the United States can have." —- quote from Richard Nixon in 1964 while campaigning for presidential candidate Barry Goldwater.

Three simple phrases could have saved President Richard Nixon's presidency:

"I lied; I covered up; and I am sorry."

Remembering one simple universal law of infidelity could have saved Bill Clinton and Jesse Jackson from public embarrassment: "The No-Tell Motel Will Tell!"

If you study the fall of leaders from grace, there are many reasons for their collapse: for some it is sex, for others it is greed and for more it is blind ambition; yet all of these issues are merely symptoms—the root cause is usually PRIDE. Pride has destroyed more leaders than any other fatal flaw. Believing that one is terminally unique is usually terminal. Believing that the rules and the laws of God do not apply to us is the beginning of our downfall. God has two basic laws for leaders: "Your sins will find you out," and "What is done in the darkness will surely come to light."

It is so easy to fall in love with our human abilities and talents. We can be blessed with good looks, charm, wit, talent and energy…all of which can give us a false sense of invincibility. The greater the gifts a leader possesses, the greater the risk of him or her falling into the trap of narcissism and self-worship.

The best example of how pride can destroy a leader is the Biblical story of a great king named Nebuchadnezzar. He was the king of the most powerful empire on earth at the time: Babylon. He built a structure that was one of the Seven Wonders of the World. He was arrogant, he was confident, he was powerful, he was brutal and he possessed absolute control of his world.

One night he had a dream that disturbed him and he pulled together the brain trust of his kingdom to explain the meaning of his dream, but no one could.

He was led to a humble, yet wise young man, full of Dunamis, named Daniel. Daniel told him about the dream, not only describing the details, but also interpreting their meaning.

The following record is kept in the book of Daniel chapter

4:4-37.

To summarize the story, Daniel tells the king that he dreamed of a great tree that was cut down to its stump. Then messengers appear in the dream and say:

" 'Let him be drenched with the dew of heaven and let him live with the animals. Let his mind be crazed like that of a wild beast until seven times have passed.' The messengers announce the decision, that the holy ones declare the verdict; so that the living may know that the MOST HIGH is sovereign over the kingdoms of men and gives them to anyone he wishes and sets over them the lowliest of men."

The king told Daniel that that was indeed the dream he had and he wanted to know its meaning.

Daniel said to the king,

> *"**The tree that you saw** that was so great and tall and was cut down to the stump **is you, O king; you are that tree**. You have become great and strong; your greatness has grown until it reaches the sky and your domain extends to distant parts of the earth.*

> *The Most High God, O King, has judged against you. Because of your **arrogance** and **PRIDE** you will be driven from your people and will live with the wild animals; you will eat grass like the cattle and be drenched with the dew of the land for seven times. **This will happen for seven times UNTIL YOU ACKNOWLEDGE THAT THE MOST HIGH GOD IS SOVEREIGN OVER THE KINGDOMS OF MEN AND GIVES THEM TO ANYONE HE WISHES.***

> *Therefore, O great King, accept my advice and my counsel, renounce your sins by doing what is right and turn from your evil by being kind to the poor and the oppressed. If you do this then your prosperity will return."*

Twelve months later (meaning the King ignored Daniel's council to repent of his pride), as King Nebuchadnezzar was walking on the rooftop of the royal palace of Babylon, he said to himself,

> *"Is not this the great Babylon **I** have built as the royal residence, by **MY** mighty power and for the glory of **MY** majesty?"*

While the words were still on his lips, a voice came from heaven saying,

> *"This is what is decreed for you, King Nebuchadnezzar: your royal authority has been taken from you. You will be driven from your people and will live with the wild animals. You will eat grass like the cattle until **<u>YOU ACKNOWLEDGE</u>** that the Most High is Sovereign over the kingdoms of men and gives them to anyone he wishes."*

Immediately, the King lost his mind and lived like a wild animal: his hair grew like wild feathers on his head and his nails grew long and curled like cork screws.

Have you ever lived like that; completely out of control? Has there ever been a time in your life when you completely gave in to your lusts and appetites for self-indulgent, unchecked narcissism—existing like a wild animal, sleeping with anyone, drinking everything, mad, rebellious and insane?

If money was the answer to life, then why did Howard Hughes, one of the richest businessmen of our time, live his last days like a like a crazed circus freak: long white hair, long finger and toenails that grew like corkscrews, forcing everyone around him to wear surgical masks and gloves before they could touch him? He kept jars of his urine and other body wastes on display in his cave-like, air-tight, sound-proof room.

If power was the answer to life, then why did the main character in the movie classic *Citizen Kane* waste his last breath before dying, whispering, "Rose Bud," the name of his boyhood sleigh (a symbol of his lost innocence and childhood)?

Maybe this book was written just for you as God's last attempt to touch your heart and quicken your soul. Maybe your great tree is to be cut down soon to the stump, and you are to be driven from your people to live like a wild animal, if you are not willing to humbly admit that God is God, that you can do nothing without His divine Holy Spirit and the power which flows from that relationship, called Dunamis.

God will try two ways to get your attention. First, He will try His best to draw you to Himself. He tries to draw you through love, patience, through the preaching of a pastor, the words from a loved one, a song on the radio or the reading of a book. If God cannot draw you to Himself, He is then very capable of driving you to Him. Trials and tribulations can be used to get your attention. The longer we ignore the signs, the stronger the trials become.

Here is my heartfelt *caveat*: whatever you love more than God, worship like a god, seek after like a god and adore more than God is an intellectual idol. God will reach out and remind you that there is no other God but Him, and until you acknowledge Him as sovereign He will dry up the land, send locusts like he did to Egypt and pestilence upon you like he did to Job. Just ask the Pharaoh who wouldn't let the Hebrews out of bondage. God kept turning up the dial of plagues until He finally touched the thing Pharaoh loved most: his first-born son.

Friends, I speak from experience. There was a dark time when I left my faith due to my anger with God for all of the abuse and rejection that I experienced in my childhood. I was so full of venom and vinegar; I was no good to anyone. For years I held onto this bitterness and anger and eventually tried to find comfort in sex. This searching led me into the arms of a woman other than my wife, a woman who lived in our upscale housing development. The consequences were ugly: everybody in my company knew about it, my wife and I separated, my kids lost respect for me—and it was hell.

God kept trying to get my attention to repent of my sin. He used my Pastor, my wife and others who kept trying to reach my cold and dead heart. I was like a wild animal, rebellious and out of control. I kept saying to myself, "I work hard, I am a millionaire, this woman loves me, she makes me feel good, so why won't people just leave us alone?"

* * *

One of the things I really enjoyed was coaching boys in little league football. I coached my two-step sons, Jason and Cedric, to undefeated seasons; I worked with NFL players and coaches and loved everything about the game. I was now going to coach my youngest son, Christopher. For the first time in his life he was going to finally get to play for Dad. He had watched

Dunamis *Transcendent Leadership Power for the 21st Century*

and waited for years as I coached hundreds of other boys—and now it was his turn.

All my teams that won championships were given rings with their names, their teams and their numbers on it. Christopher couldn't wait to earn his ring.

On the first play of the season, Christopher, wanting so much to please me, took a hard hit to the head and laid motionless on the football field. He didn't get up, he didn't move, he just lay there. I knew something was terribly wrong and I ran onto the field. You must understand what Chris meant to me: I believed, in my twisted mind, that he was my redemption; I was going to give to him everything I didn't get because I did not have a father. But in reality I was giving him everything, except what he really needed, which was a father of character and godliness.

As I walked over to him, he looked up through his helmet with a tear in his eye and said, "Daddy, I can't feel my body." My son was paralyzed from the chest down. The ambulance was called and the truck came onto the field and they put my baby on the stretcher and drove him to the hospital.

I saw the doctors cut the uniform and his helmet off his body and watched in horror as the doctor probed my 10-year-old son's limp body for feeling. He had no feeling from his mid-chest down to his toes. The doctors were very concerned about his spinal cord, but the swelling was so severe they couldn't analyze the extent and the scope of the damage.

As I stared down at my paralyzed son I realized that his physical paralysis was an extension of my own spiritual paralysis.

At ten, I was paralyzed spiritually for not having a father, and my son at ten was paralyzed physically because of his

82

immoral father. My worst nightmare was being realized. The one thing in life I loved more than life, itself, had been touched by tragedy. All my money, fame and power meant nothing.

God finally had my full-undivided attention. I hadn't prayed in five years, I hadn't attended church in over seven years, but all I could do now was drop to my knees and look up to heaven from which my help comes.

I knelt beside my son's hospital bed and prayed for the first time in five years. I confessed all my sins and asked God to forgive me and not to judge my son for my pride, arrogance and disobedience. For three long hours I prayed until sweat ran down my face. I walked to the restroom and when I returned my son whispered softly, "Daddy, I can move my Big toe." Little by little and hour by hour feeling slowly came back to his body, one toe and one finger at a time, until his entire body fully recovered. I cried and thanked God for the miracle. The doctors were amazed by his recovery and put his head in a harness just as a precautionary measure. I had witnessed the power of Dunamis first-hand. I would never be the same again. My son and I were given a second chance and just five years later, on April 18, 2002, we were on Air Force One, holding hands and WALKING together aboard the President's private airplane, thanking God for His mercy and kindness. My son will be with me as we open the Dunamis Institute for advanced leadership development in Maui, Hawaii, a ministry to share God's healing power with world leaders.

* * *

In Daniel chapter 4:34-37

> *King Nebuchadnezzar says, "At the end of the seven times I
> raised my eyes toward heaven and my sanity was restored.
> Then I praised the MOST HIGH GOD; I honored and
> glorified Him who lives forever. His dominion is an eternal
> dominion; His kingdom endures from generation to genera-
> tion. All the people of the earth are regarded as nothing. He
> does as he pleases with the powers of heaven and the peoples
> of the earth. No one can hold back His hand or say to
> Him: What have you done? At the same time that my sanity
> was restored, my honor and splendor were returned to me for
> the glory of my kingdom. My advisers and nobles sought me
> out, and I was restored to my throne and became even greater
> than before. Now I, Nebuchadnezzar, praise and exalt and
> glorify the true KING of heaven, because everything He does
> is right and all His ways are just. **AND ALL THOSE
> WHO WALK IN PRIDE HE IS ABLE TO HUMBLE***."

The above Bible story that I just shared is my story. My
pride and arrogance led to all of my downfalls and failures in life.
It wasn't until my world had been rocked and I was knocked off
my self-exalted throne that I lifted my eyes toward heaven—and
then did my sanity return to me. It is never too late to come
back home. I don't care what you have done, how far you have
strayed or how lost you feel, God is waiting for you to come to
your senses and return to Him. He and I wait for you with open
and loving arms. If you need to talk, please call me or my staff
toll free at 1-866-4-DUNAMS or email us at:
ron@thedunamisinstitute.com

We all go through something, to become something else, to

do something of lasting value with our lives. Remember, God uses greatly those who have been wounded very deeply. It is not the falling down, but the staying down; so if you can look up, then you can get up, so never give up. Just ask my son Christopher.

How to Receive the Gift of Dunamis

Leaders, I pray that you can experience the power that God wants to flow through you to do the impossible and perform the supernatural. Whether it is like Moses having to lead difficult and ungrateful people, or, like Mother Teresa, being called to love the unlovable.

If you are in need of a renewal of strength, faith and a revival of spirit, if you truly want to receive and unleash Dunamis in your life, begin by saying this prayer with me:

"Lord, I have lost my way. How do I get back to an intimate relationship with you? I have tried living life on my own terms, in my own strength, with my own plans and dissatisfaction and emptiness have been the result. Please forgive me for my prideful heart, forgive me for my selfish soul and restore to me the joy and the meaning of life. I need You, Lord, and I am lost without You. Please receive me as Your humbled child in need of Your love, mercy, compassion, peace and joy.

"I rededicate my life to serving Your will by glorifying Your goodness and mercy. Use my talents, gifts and resources for Your service to uplift the human spirit and to heal the broken minded.

"I will lift up the name of Jesus Christ, but I ask that You fill me with Your Holy Spirit and unleash Dunamis in my life and the life of my loved ones. I want my last days on this earth to count for You. Let love, joy, peace, patience, kindness, goodness, faithfulness, humility and self-control radiate from my life as I lead and follow others. For I now know that I have this treasure in my fragile earthen vessel, that the Excellency of the POWER may be of God and not of me. Let Your light so shine through me that others may know of Your love and Your mercy. Help me to transcend the difficulties of life with faith, confidence and dignity knowing that You are always with me even until the end of the age. I ask this prayer with faith and thanksgiving in the name of our Lord and Savior Jesus Christ, AMEN."

Developing a humble and grateful attitude toward God is the first step in building a strong Character Quotient.

* * *

What we leaders also need today, to maintain a strong character quotient, is a Personal Accountability Partner: someone we can be totally honest and naked with, someone who is not afraid to tell us the truth, someone who will not enable our dysfunctionality. Power without accountability is a recipe for self-destruction. When Bill Clinton was involved with Monica he couldn't be honest with anyone. He lied to his wife, his staff, his advisers, his lawyers and his friends. He had no one to hold him accountable.

Billy Graham, the great evangelist, as a policy is never alone with a woman—he will always have a male member of his staff with him. Why? Accountability. As the Bible states, "Faithful are the wounds of a friend." Personal accountability is the guard dog for our character.

Chapter 5

Dunamis for Organizations and Teams

Cynthia Archer, M.S.
Organizational Development and Analysis
Case Western Reserve University
Co-Founder of the Dunamis Institute

"Where there is no vision, the people perish..."

People and organizations are becoming more and more reliant on the computer, Internet, web-based communication, cellular phones, and other technologies, which has resulted in less physical human interaction. Many organizations and social agencies are currently experiencing periods of strong internal turmoil, pressure and change in the environment due to these sudden technological developments, global competition, and changing attitudes among the employees. The challenge for leaders is to create and develop an organization that can excel in the rapidly approaching future.

More specific challenges for today's leaders involve how to:
- Transform for tomorrow, while leading today
- Manage an uncontrollable discovery or learning process
- Lead to an unclear destination
- Deal with disruption
- Confront the need for personal change

The key to the challenges facing today's leadership is to balance the three foundations (Novelty, Continuity, and Transition) that make for a healthy organization.

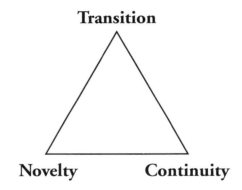

- **Novelty** - Unexpected newness and the generation of a truly value-driven organization where one's ideas and hopes are aligned with, or embedded in the organization's agendas and activities.

- **Continuity** - Maintenance of day-to-day activity reinforcing aspects of the organization's culture that ensures the accomplishment of core tasks at desired levels of performance.

- **Transition** - Managing or leading a desired or planned change—getting from A to B. It is the conscious mobilization of an organization's people and resources toward a more effective diverse state.

Life-Cycle of Organizational Change

In order to effectively begin balancing Novelty, Continuity and Transition, a leader must view her organization as a living and breathing entity. Just like any living organism, it grows through a life cycle. All living organisms have iterations (or change phases) as they experience challenges, crises and obstacles.

The five phases that typify most organizations' change cycle are: Honeymoon, Doubt and Confusion, Clarification, Unification and Maturation. The focus of this chapter will be on the first two phases, because most organizations rarely survive the complexities and trauma of phase two. Organizations frequently remain stuck in the quagmire of Doubt and Confusion for decades.

Honeymoon Phase

Phase one is called the "Honeymoon Phase." This phase lasts between 3-6 months, and during this phase the members of the group are full of excitement, energy and enthusiasm for the new enterprise. Celebratory activities and events with balloons, banners, music, team logos, t-shirts, hats, guest speakers and ribbon-cutting ceremonies are typical during this phase. Events such as the wedding ceremony, the opening of a new strip mall, the dedication of a new restaurant, the consecration of a new church and the first day of college, all share the ceremonial excitement of phase one.

During this phase leaders are basically cheerleaders. They fan the flames of hope and promise, and stoke the furnace with words of possibility. Even the most cynical become, at least, for a brief moment, cautiously optimistic.

It is amazing what one hears during phase one. Here are a few examples of sayings repeated by leaders during kick-off ceremonies:

1. "We're going to boldly go where no team has gone before!"
2. "Those who say it can't be done better get out of the way for those of us who are going to do it!"
3. "Either you are on the way or in the way."
4. "Who cares if the horse is blind just keep loading the wagon?"
5. "Let's get in the rowboat! We are going after Jaws, and bring the tartar sauce with a side of slaw; we are going to have lunch today!"

It is important for you, as the leader, to know that during phase one the members of the team or organization are a group and not a team. They must, therefore, be managed in order to be successful and effective because, within a short few months, all of this excitement turns into the anxiety, mistrust, and disillusionment of Phase Two: Doubt and Confusion, or Separation Anxiety.

How do leaders tell the difference between a group and a team? Review the chart below.

WORK GROUP	TEAM
• Strong, focused leader	• Shared leadership roles
• Individual accountability	• Individual and Mutual Accountability
• Group's purpose same as organization's mission	• Specific purpose that team itself delivers
• Individual work-products	• Collective work-products
• Runs efficient meetings; focuses on communication	• Encourages open-ended discussions and active problem-solving
• Measures its effectiveness indirectly by influence on others	• Measures performance by assessing collective work-products
• Discusses, decides, delegates	• Discusses, decides, and does real work together

* From: The *Discipline of Teams* by J. Katzenbach & D Smith, <u>HBR</u>. *March-April, 1993*

Doubt and Confusion Phase

The Doubt and Confusion (or Separation Anxiety) Phase can last from 12 months to 12 years. According to Ron Archer's <u>On Teams</u>, eighty percent of the change efforts that fail, do so during this phase.

The leader knows when he is in stage two because there are four cries that echo from the group:

1. "That's not my job"
2. "That's not my problem"
3. "That's not my fault"
4. "Let's go back to how things used to be" and "I don't need anyone but myself"

The human organization becomes an interesting entity when it is faced with change, crisis or challenge; it is one of the few organisms that would rather embrace a known pain than to pursue an unknown promise. When a movement or an organization experiences the trials and tribulations of phase two, the population falls into the 20/60/20 separation-anxiety bell curve. Twenty percent of the population becomes Winners, sixty percent of the population becomes Wanderers and the last twenty percent of the population becomes toxic Whiners.

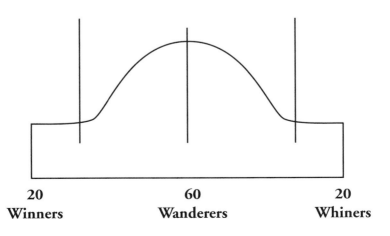

20	60	20
Winners	**Wanderers**	**Whiners**

The Toxic Whiner

Whiners are the chronic complainers and doomsayers. They are the "I told ya so" group. Whiners are so invested in yesterday that they fear what tomorrow may bring. A great example is the story of Moses and the Exodus. Moses explains to his team the great vision he has been given of the new paradigm–a place filled with milk and honey, where each member will have his and her own fig tree, flowing streams of water, green pastures for grazing flocks; a new land where each will be free to pursue life and liberty as a new nation and new people. Half-way through the journey, after a few years of walking in the dry, hot desert of despair, the quitters begin to hold meetings. They reach a conclusion among themselves that it was better to be slaves in Egypt than to die like animals in the desert chasing some "make believe" promised land that they had yet to see.

Now listen folks: we all have bad days; but all the time, everyday and at every meeting or function? That's the whiner for you. Just as an ill-behaved child might throw a tantrum to get a piece of candy, Whiners either get their way or they scream and cry until someone gives in to their demands. The danger of giving in to the Whiner is that it sets a behavior standard for the group that demonstrates how to get what you want—the 'squeaky wheel gets the grease' syndrome. Whiners have a mental dysfunction called "learned helplessness," according to the research of Martin Seligman of the University of Pennsylvania. They associate pain and rejection with effort, so they stop trying to achieve, altogether. They become skillful at infecting others around them with their pain, misery and negativity.

An example of learned helplessness is the process of how circus elephants are trained and controlled to perform tricks. The first thing the trainer has to do is to convince the pachyderm that to escape from this life of captivity is impossible. The circus will take a newborn calf, after it is weaned from its mother, and bring it to the training department. Trainers attach a heavy leg iron to the calf's front and hind legs, and attach the leg iron to a heavy chain that is attached to an iron stake that is imbedded in 500lbs of solid concrete. The young calf tries for months to pull away. The bracelet has small spikes inside, so as the elephant pulls at the chain, the spikes cause more and more pain. The pressure and pain teaches the elephant two lessons: escape from the bracelet is impossible and it is very painful to keep trying. At some point in the conditioning process the elephant reaches a state of learned helplessness and it stops trying to escape—even after the heavy chain is taken off and all that remains is the bracelet. As long as the elephant sees and feels the bracelet, it does not try to escape or resist. It has learned to be helpless. The elephant has been psychologically broken.

How many people do you know who have learned to be helpless? They have great ideas, but they always talk themselves out of putting the ideas into practice. They have ideas like going back to college to finish their degrees, applying to graduate school, starting their own business, or going back to church. They have been so conditioned to believe that they can't climb out of their ruts that they don't even try. They go to their graves with their best music left unplayed and unheard, leaving behind a legacy of "woulda, coulda, and shoulda."

As they see others climbing ahead of them, reaching their dreams, they become jealous and envious. Envy is defined, according to Ron Archer's On Teams, as wanting what others have, yet being unwilling to do what they had to do to achieve it. Jealousy, once again according to Archer, is defined as believing that others don't deserve what they have. Whiners make a life of putting up roadblocks and discouraging others. They are mean-spirited put-down artists who will try to sabotage anyone who dares to climb. And if a climber falls, the Whiners will try to convince him to stop climbing and settle with them in the valley of despair.

You can readily recognize a Whiner from the following behavior patterns:

1. Driven for the attention from others (Attention-Starved)
2. Obsession with gaining power and control (Control Freak)
3. Preoccupation with revenge (Petty)
4. Lives a facade; dishonest and deceitful (Phony)
5. Excessive perfectionists, rigid, inflexible (Bull-Headed)
6. Closed-minded to change and new ideas (Mr. Know-It-All)
7. Cowardly; retreats from life's challenges (Hit-and-Run Driver)
8. Blames others for own faults; excuse maker, irresponsible (Whiner)
9. Hides behind tough image to mask a lack of confidence (Wizard of OZ)
10. Has thoughts of worthlessness and shame (Wounded Soul)

Some Dunamis leaders can actually start off as Whiners. If this profile fits you, don't despair: you might still be a candidate for greatness. The key will be how the Whiner responds to the offer of Dunamis.

The Wanderer

The Wanderer is an interesting behavior model. The Wanderer is a chameleon-like person who only works and strives as long as he has an audience. The goal is to do as little as possible while still pleasing everyone around him. The wanderer loves to socialize and hang around the water cooler, the teachers' lounge and the cafeteria to listen to and pass on gossip. Wanderers are often skilled politicians. Wanderers want to be liked both by Winners and Whiners. When they are around Winners they talk about having a winning strategy and the importance of the work ethic and reaching goals. When they are around Whiners, they complain about the workload and how unfair things are. They simply won't commit to either camp.

Instead of working, they want to sing songs around the campfire and roast marshmallows. They are especially skilled at changing the subject if it will cause conflict within the group. Wanderers tend to over-promise and under-deliver on commitments, and are easily hurt by criticism and direct confrontation. They do their best to avoid both.

Here is a behavior profile for the Wanderer:

1. Wants to be liked and will try to please both Winners and Whiners
2. Values stability over change
3. Values security over risk-taking
4. Would rather talk about winning than prepare for and work to win
5. Great dreamers, but poor implementers
6. Confuses activity with accomplishment (always appears to be busy)
7. Arrives on-time and leaves on-time, nothing extra
8. Will never volunteer to lead a project
9. Only wins if someone constantly pushes them; needs constant motivation
10. Offers compliance, not commitment

With a caring coach who knows how to connect with them personally and hold them accountable, Wanderers can make great team members. Wanderers are involved in the search for significance. They want to know how important they are to you as a coach. To motivate them, use the EVM ("Explore, Validate and Motivate") approach to coaching, and SMART method of goal setting (more on the SMART method below).

Wanderers don't care how much you know until they know how much you care about them as human beings. They are most often "High Context" personalities and function as social technical creatures. The EVM method is the best way to connect and to motivate them to achieve peak performance: Explore, Validate, Motivate.

The EVM Method

When coaching a Wanderer, you must explore with empathy to find understanding by asking lots of open-ended questions that allow them to vent until they are spent. When Wanderers are in a funk, you have to remind them of past successes and how great they will feel when they reach the next step in the work plan—and how proud the team will be of them. You must also validate their feelings. You don't have to agree with them, but you must validate their right to feel as they do. Simply put, Wanderers just want to feel that you understand their position.

Once Wanderers feel validated they will run through a wall for you. When offering correction to a Wanderer, please handle the exchange with care. Use the following approach:

1. Focus comments on behaviors that can be changed, not on personal traits that cannot.
2. Maintain their self worth at all times by offering honest and encouraging options.
3. Follow up with a lunch once a month to check on progress.

The Smart Method

Lastly, you motivate by using the SMART method. To keep a Wanderer on task give them direction and goals that follow the SMART concept. SMART calls for making goals and objectives, which are:

- Specific
- Measurable
- Attainable
- Relevant/Realistic
- Timely

Remember you can't push a Wanderer across the street, but you can lead them around the world.

The Winner

Winners are task-driven and achievement-oriented. They want to do things right the first time and every time. Multi-skilled and multi-talented, Winners want to be leaders—and they want to turn other team members into Winners. They want to win, but win the right way.

They equally value the what and the how. They are value-driven, but with an open heart. They have failed in life, but they have become better, not bitter: a Winner not a Whiner, a contender not a pretender. They view winning as a way of life. Their theme for winning says "incremental improvement is better than postponed perfection," and, accordingly, they take little steps each day to inch closer to their dreams. By the yard it's hard, but by the inch it's a cinch. They do what they can, with what they have, with where they are right now. And they seek to improve from there, day in and day out. Thus, no matter how small the steps they are taking may seem, they remain committed to getting better everyday. They aim for perfection and catch excellence along the way.

Here is a profile of the Winner:

1. Dunamis motivated, task-driven, but compassionate
2. Openly supports others and cooperates; will listen to opposing views
3. Coaches, teaches and motivates others by own example
4. Refreshed by change and challenges
5. Takes personal responsibility for mistakes and will work to correct them
6. Shares credit for reaching the summit
7. Makes others feel important
8. Confident and Courageous; wants to be respected first and liked second
9. Loves truth and honesty; Pragmatic and Realistic
10. Conducts a Ruthless-Self Examination before confronting others

What turns a Whiner or Wanderer into a Winner? The unleashing of DUNAMIS.

Take Peter, the chief of the disciples, the man who swore he would never deny his leader. He boldly pronounced that others might deny Jesus, but that he never would. When the rubber hit the road, he denied his leader not once, not twice, but thrice. Talk about over-promising and under-delivering!

Then he just lost it: he quit and hid out and felt worthless. Now, how did this same guy go from such a low point in his life to the leader who, in one day, and in the face of great personal danger, convinced 3,000 men to risk their lives and join his cause?...But join they did, and the movement that would change the world had begun to pick up steam. This all happened when Peter came to the end of his own strength. He admitted his wrong-doing and weakness and emptied himself of himself to be filled with the mercy, love and hope of a compassionate God.

* * *

As I read the Bible, I was lead to he Old Testament, II Chronicles where I read about the riches of King Solomon. He was building an empire and a great temple and wanted God to bless it and to keep His presence there. Something I read there caught my attention. It was in the 7th, 13th and 14th chapters, when the Almighty is speaking to Solomon about the requests he has made. God answers Solomon's questions by saying: "If I shut up the heaven and there be no rain. If I send the locusts to devour the land and if I send pestilence among my people."

That seemed so cold to this author. Solomon is asking God for a blessing and He comes back with the horrible crop and weather report. But as I read the passage over and over again several times, the progression of the forecast made so much sense to me. If there is no rain, we experience a drought and the crop yield is going to be poor. Then locusts would come and devour the crops that were not completely damaged by the drought.

First no water, now no food, and the people who survived those calamities would obviously face the threat of pestilence.

Ever have a year like that? When revenues and earnings dry up and the taxes, debts, interest and expenses, like locusts, start eating up your cash reserves and investments? You think things can't get any worse and then somebody in the family contracts a mysterious illness that the doctors can't figure out. The medical bills escalate and you are almost destroyed. You're thinking: "What have I done to deserve all this?"

The author has learned when life wants to get your attention, it starts with loving whispers, nudges and winks. If we continually ignore the signs, then it will send a drought, some locusts and some strange rash that keeps spreading over your body with green and purple spots. If life can't draw you to deep reflection and introspection, then life can drive you to your knees through the crush of events and circumstances. It's like the old car mechanic who says, "You can either pay me for an oil change now or you can pay me more for an engine overhaul later. Either way you are going to pay me, but the cost will totally be up to you."

News reports across the country reported that after September 11th, church attendance went up over 300% and has been holding steady since. Obviously we are not saying God planned for the attack on America, but as we said earlier, life is a volatile mixture of the unexplained blended with the unforeseen. When life happens to us—and it will—how we respond is the key to our happiness. As earlier stated, trouble is with us right now, and it is always just leaving or coming back around. September 11th was merely a reminder of how little control we really have over what happens to us. But as Rudy Giuliani and other Dunamis-filled leaders have shown us, we have complete control over how we respond to the things that life hands us.

Appreciative Inquiry: A Methodology of Positive Change

As a leader, your challenge is to create an environment that will transform your Whiners and Wanderers into Winners, which, when accomplished, will springboard you out of stage two. Through a methodology of Appreciative Inquiry (AI), organizations and teams can engage in positive interaction and active interdependence. The process of AI allows for collaborative efforts to affirm past and present strengths, and potentials to perceive those things that give life (health, vitality, excellence) to living systems and to discover and design new potentials and possibilities for the future.

What is Appreciative Inquiry? According to Dr. David L Cooperrider, Professor at Case Western Reserve University, Appreciative Inquiry (AI) is "the co-evolutionary search for the best in people, their organization, and the relevant world around them." It involves discovering those factors that give life to an organization, envisioning new opportunities, building a consensus of an ideal or vision through dialogue. This, in turn, results in the creation of momentum, energy and passion to construct and help move the organization to the ideal future through collaboration, innovation and action.

Appreciative Inquiry engages whole systems in a process of "unconditional positive questions" to redirect human organization toward a positive theory of change. AI involves an organization-wide analysis and invites every stakeholder—including customers, partners, community, suppliers—to the AI adventure, which flows through what is referred to as the Appreciative Inquiry 4-D cycle:*

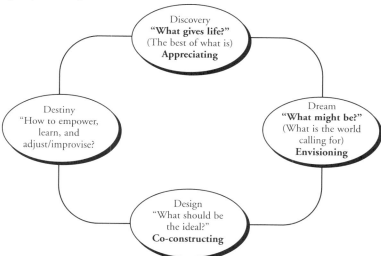

Discovery - Appreciating the best of what is through a series of questions that highlight "What gives life" within the organization and mobilize a whole system inquiry into the positive change core.

Dream - Envisioning results by asking, "What might be?", "What is the world calling us to become?" in order to create a clear, results-oriented vision, and a higher purpose through the illumination of now discovered potential.

Design - Collectively constructing or co-constructing positive images of the organization's future through creating possible propositions of the ideal organization by asking, "What should be the ideal?"

*From: Cooperrider, D., Whitney, D. and Stavros, J., <u>The Appreciative Inquiry Handbook</u> (2003), Lakeshore Communications, Euclid, OH. (used by permission)

Destiny - Sustaining and strengthening the affirmative capability of the whole system, enabling it to build hope and momentum around a deep purpose by asking, "How to empower, learn and adjust / improvise?" Destiny involves delivery on the new images of the future organization or system.

To encourage the best possible chance for success within an organization, relative to any evolutionary change, it is imperative that the AI process is sanctioned and endorsed by the positive, total commitment and signature from the executive leadership. In 1996, GTE Telops (making up 80 Percent of GTE's 67,000 employees) began the AI adventure, creating a momentum within the organization that ignited a grassroots movement that, in turn, revolutionized the whole organization. Tom White, President at the time, replied with no hesitation: "Yes, and what I see in this meeting: zealots, people with a mission and passion for creating the new GTE. Count me in. I'm your number one recruit, number one zealot."

Fourteen months later, based on significant and measurable changes in stock prices, morale survey measures, quality/customer relations, union management relations and so on, GTE's whole system change initiative won the 1997 ASTD (American Society for Training and Development) Award for best organization-change program in the country.

The Discovery Phase in More Detail

AI is designed to engage, involve and ignite whole systems, or organizations, and families in an exciting adventure towards a new and positive revolution. It is a tool for connecting to the transformational power of the positive change core within the organization. It invites employees, departments and executive leaders within a team or organization to hope, dream, imagine, innovate, generate stories, and create momentum and passion to change by asking four foundational appreciative questions, such as the following:

- Describe a high point experience in your team/organization, a time when you were most alive and engaged.

- Without being modest, tell me what do you value most about yourself, your work, and your team/organization?

- What are the core factors that give life to your team/organization that without these factors your organization would not be the same?

- You have three wishes, what would enhance the health and vitality of your team/organization?

The author adapted these four foundational AI questions to assist Burlington Northern & Sante Fe Railroad's Industrial Products Department with their teams and customer relations processes, as follows:

1. Looking at your entire experience at BNSF, reflect for a moment on a "high point" or a "peak experience." Now tell us about when you felt most alive, most involved and most excited about your participation on a team or a team project. Include:

What made the experience exciting?
Who were the most significant people involved?
Why were they significant?
What was it about your role that made the experience exciting?

2. What do you value about:

   A. Yourself (Don't be humble)?

   B. The nature of your work?

   C. BNSF?

3. What are the core factors that give vitality and life to Industrial Products teams and teamwork?

4. Think about your role. How have you helped BNSF to achieve customer satisfaction?

5. In 2001, we were introduced to the Strategic Initiatives wheel, which hinged on five priorities: Growth; Service; Ease of Doing Business; Efficiency and People. At the core of this wheel are our customers who should benefit the most from improvements in our business operations through these initiatives. Five years from now, imagine opening the Wall Street Journal and BNSF is recognized as the industry leader for overall customer satisfaction. List three things that would make this possible.

   A. BNSF's customers are raving about how they

have not just been satisfied, but their expectations have been exceeded. List three things you did to delight them, making them "raving fans."

Such AI questions will help you and your people to brainstorm possible topics (For more on the Discovery Phase, see Whitney, et. al: *Encyclopedia of Positive Questions, Vol. One, (2002)*, Lakeshore Communications, Euclid, Ohio). Topic selection is the first step in the Appreciative Inquiry process. A careful, thoughtful and informed choice of topics is important because it defines the scope of the inquiry and provides the framework for subsequent interviews and data collection.

The topics can range from technical processes, human dynamics, to customer relations, cultural themes, teamwork, market trends, etc. When considering topics, there should be no more than five: they should be phrased in affirmative terms and they should be what people want to see "grow."

The topics generated from the foundational questions are then used to create an interview questionnaire or protocol to further and more specifically explore the values, peak experiences and wishes for the organization, as well as new, more compelling images of the team's or organization's future.

Note: in this methodology of introducing positive change, the parallels to Dunamis Power…particularly the power of asking positive questions.

Organizational Dunamis At Work

After the topics, which give life to the organization have been chosen, the following is an example of the creation of the Ideal *Organization of the Future*.

Overview

"On behalf of all the people of your current organization, I am pleased to present the first *Appreciative Inquiry(AI)* report—The Ideal Organization of the Future.

My hope is that this report serves to invite every member of the organization with the opportunity to think strategically and imaginatively about 'our common vision for the *Ideal Organization of the Future.*' The report will provide inspirational pictures and memorable moments of many of the strengths of the organization when it is operating at its very best. It must be acknowledged that there is an undeniable positive quality about the report. Some of it stems from the nature of the questions that were asked in the interviews. But, equally important, much of it comes from a real sense of optimism that fuels the company and its prospects for the future. I, too, found myself really energized and excited about the organization's future when people dare to make their imaginations realities."

How This Document Was Put Together

This analysis was constructed from interviews with 6 people comprising the leadership team and the employees. The foundational questions used in the interviews (which lasted 1-2 hours each) were spawned from a 3-day workshop on *Appreciative Inquiry* held in October. During the workshop the following three topics surfaced as topics to be explored in order to enhance and strengthen the organization:

- Shared Ownership and Commitment
- Sense of Community
- Servant Leadership

The interviews were designed to explore these topics in several ways. For example, when have you felt a sense of community or sense of family within your organization? Why did you feel that sense of community or family? What things might your organization do to further instill and strengthen a sense of family/community?

On the basis of the interviews, the data was collected first from the leadership, then the employees. This report is a summary overview for the *Ideal Organization of the Future* and attempts to discover ideals that are common throughout the organization. In terms of the analysis, the interview responses were typed and grouped together by questions. The next step was to code each comment to discover, for example: What were the most important factors that create, maintain and strengthen a sense of community/family? Examples and quotes that related to the theme sense of community/family were grouped together in an attempt to put words to the ***topic-ideals***. What do people within the organization really mean when speaking about a sense of community/family? What are the people really saying is the *ideal*? I figured that if I did my homework well, the *topic-ideals*, as written, would resonate strongly with what people want the organization to be.

Two things are important to keep in mind when reading through this report. First, these *topic-ideals* are fashioned from people's actual experiences. There are many examples of each of the ideals (see actual quotes). Thus, the topic-ideals express the corporate culture of the organization as we understand it from the appreciation of proven strengths.

Secondly, the statements also represent a bold extension of these strengths – a focused vision to which people are saying they aspire as an organization. The *topic-ideals* are stated in the present ideal based upon experiences when individuals and the organiza-tion were at their best. I invite you to use this document as a resource to help you think seriously about what you want your own organization to be like in the future.

How To Use This Document: A Template
The most thorough approach would be as follows:

1. Read the summary at the beginning of each section to get a feeling for the topic-ideal. Ask yourself: if we could be this way all the time, would I want it?

2. Read each of the sample quotes to get an idea of what people actually talked about. Ask yourself: do these quotes illustrate the topic ideal? Do you have examples from your own experience, which illustrate the way things could be in the ideal? What are those illustrations?

3. Read through the analysis. Ask yourself: does the analysis sound plausible? What else would you add to the analysis?

The Ideal Organization of the Future

Interview Protocol
(Discovery Phase)

Name _____

Title _____

Date _____

Group _____

Years of Service _____

Interviewed by ___*Cynthia D. Archer*_____

Opening

Thank you for agreeing to this interview. The objective of this interview is to appreciate or value the best of "What Is" in your organization and dream and design the "Ideal Organization of the Future."

The information you provide will assist me in exploring the untapped possibilities for a more vital, successful and effective organization. Your experiences, stories, and moments of success are the energy that is needed to give birth to the "Ideal Organization of the Future." The interview will take about one hour. The interview will tend to focus on the organization when it is operating at its best in the following topic areas:

1. Shared Ownership and Commitment
2. Sense of Community
3. Servant Leadership

A. Shared Ownership And Commitment

Organizations work best when the employees at all levels share a basic, common vision in relation to the organization's core mission, intent and direction. When employees know the big picture or the vision, they often experience a feeling of purpose, pride, significance, and unity.

1. In your mind, what is the common mission or purpose that unites everyone in this organization?

2. Tell me about an experience when you felt most committed to your organization's vision or mission, and you and the employees felt a sense of ownership, purpose, pride, and unity.

3. Think about the future. What could your organization do more of to create a shared vision of the future and heighten the sense of ownership and commitment at all levels?

B. Sense Of Community/Family

An organization becomes the desired workplace for people when there is a sense of community, where every member of the organization feels valued, where information is shared to a point that the members take ownership, where opinions are respected, where people think, feel and act as a cohesive community in the furtherance of common goals.

4. Think of a time when you felt a sense of community/sense of family within your organization.
   • A time when you felt a sense of ownership

5. Why did you feel that sense of family and ownership?

6. Think about the future of your organization. What things might you and your organization do to further instill and strengthen a sense of community/family?

C. Servant Leadership

Servant leadership is about how leaders get things done in organizations, by serving. It begins with the feeling that one wants to serve. Then, the servant-leader makes sure that serving the needs of others is his highest priority. By modeling the way, the servant-leader enables others to act and turn challenging opportunities into powerful successes within their organization.

7. What individual qualities do you think a servant-leader should model?

8. Tell me about a time when you have led others by serving.

9. Describe what the organization would look like when the leaders and employees are modeling servant-leadership behaviors.

During the Discovery Phase, it is important for the interviewer to record "the best quote" and "the best story" that came out of the interview. This information will be used to engage the team or organization to "go beyond what they thought was impossible and to push the creative edges of possibility to reach its greatest potential" (Dream Phase).

During the Dream Phase, the team or organization begins to envision the future based on its successful past and it begins to balance and weave meaning into continuity, novelty and transition. A typical Dream Process is to design small groups of 8-12 people who review the data from the interviews with a focus on the dream/future/miracle questions. The groups then discuss their vision of the ideal organization and scope out what would happen in the organization 3-5 years in the future. The groups prepare expressive enactments of their organizations. The enactments are encouraged to be creative, through the use of Poetry, TV Commercials, Songs, Jingles, One-act Plays etc...

The aim of Appreciative Inquiry is to help teams and organizations envision a collective, desired, future state and to carry forth the desired future state in ways which successfully "translate intentions into reality and beliefs into practice." The process then proceeds to the construction of provocative propositions based upon the topics of inquiry and the data collected. Review the proposition below.

Proposition

The "Ideal Organization of the Future" is a visionary organization with a core purpose that generates levels of commitment, unity, pride, esteem and confidence, all of which are the ingredients necessary to take risks and explore new horizons. The organization is a corporate community/family where differences are expected and respected and accomplishments are rewarded. The organization fosters an environment of servitude, whereby continuous learning becomes a continuous process fueled by the unleashing of the organization's human potential.

The Appreciative Inquiry process goes on to describe the Ideal-Type themes with illustrative quotes and stories. This information can be used as background material for building the provocative propositions.

Ideal-Type Theme #1: Shared Ownership and Commitment

The "Ideal Organization of the Future" is a visionary organization where both the leaders and the employees have established a purpose or a set of fundamental reasons for existing. Through open communication, respect of their differences, and by searching deep within the very soul of the organization, the purpose is discovered and birthed.

The core purpose then becomes so meaningful and inspirational to the people who created it that they are compelled to generate a commitment to the success of the organization—a commitment that cannot be compromised. Having purpose gives life and meaning to the human spirit within the organization and thereby drives people to constantly move toward and align with the common vision. The leaders and employees experience a feeling of pride, significance and unity as they press forward.

Through a progressive drive toward achievement and success that is consistent with the vision and purpose, the "Ideal Organization of the Future" displays a combination of shared esteem and confidence. This shared esteem and confidence then becomes the stimulus necessary for people to set goals, take risks and expand themselves and the organization to new horizons.

Sample Quotes

"In the name of God there has to be a ribbon of some kind of common saneness. If I could get people to talk and to respect each other's differences, the commonness between them will automatically surface."

"I felt most committed when SC Johnson and Son flew their three top executives to my home for a private meeting to enlist my company's services, to help their corporation out of an internal crisis. Of all the companies in the world, they selected my company to design, develop and deliver a complete organizational re-engineering process over a two-year period. They gave us the mandate to re-create their

compensation system, their coaching training program, their team assessment validation tool, and to conduct leadership development. The true test was our ability to come together as a team knowing that this was a huge project that stressed us to our limits. Confidence and commitment levels peaked as we seized it, tackled it and did it extremely well."

"Writing my first book was one of my dreams. It was a very challenging process, but I knew that the book was a very important piece of my organization's growth. Working with my wife and my ghostwriter to map out chapters and to talk about why the book would sell was all worth it the moment when I got the first draft back with a picture of myself on the cover of the book. In some capacity I felt a sense of 'we had arrived.' No matter if I died tomorrow, this book would live on forever. Somebody believed that what we, as an organization, had accomplished with other organizations was worth puting in a print and selling as book. I felt a real sense of accomplishment, commitment and awareness of our own success."

"When I made up my mind to be committed to the building of our business, I gave all my time and energy to the process. Then one day I realized that through all my hard work and my investment of sweat equity, I was part owner in the business. The business was just as much mine, as it was the owners."

"I felt most committed when we gave my mother a surprise birthday party. I wanted to make sure that everything was just right. My siblings and I divided the cost of the party between us and I delegated some of the responsibility to my sister, since we don't live in the same city. The moment of truth came and Mom was so surprised. I *was proud that it went perfect and everyone cooperated and did their part to make her party a success. It was the excitement and the sheer joy of seeing my mother happy that made it all worthwhile."*

Ideal-Type Theme #2: Sense of Community/Family

The "Ideal Organization of the Future" is a community/family where all racial and social barriers have diminished and status and economical differences have been abolished. People within the family feel valued because there is a respect for human dignity, high standards, and technical competencies.

Family members do not compete with each other, but seek opportunities to encourage and support common goals. There is no bickering about what has to be done. The question becomes "What can I do to help you?" There is such an intermingling and an interaction that when a crisis or a tragedy arises, the people within the organization open up and rally around each other to form strong bands of support, deepening that sense of community.

The organization is a community/family of lifelong learners that sees change as opportunity for growth. As change occurs, levels of communication between family members increase. The organization encourages open and clear communication as a means to build trust and honesty and activate the flow of ideas and innovations.

The organization of the future provides funding for community projects and activities. Emphasis is placed on education and community safety.

Sample Quotes

"There was a little four year old boy in our church who died of meningitis. His death brought a sense of oneness and family to our church and community. There was this pulling together of the congregation and community. We all responded as though it happened to someone within our family. It was a strange feeling, but there was a unity and cohesiveness that could not be explained. The people just wove themselves around the little boy's family. The event caused the whole community to make sure the other children were safe and that they had the necessary shots to combat meningitis."

"I value my family in that even the hardships of what a family setting can present, I know that it is my family that has helped to keep me focused, grounded, mature and whole. Sometimes, when I have felt as though I was going to fall apart, it was my family that has kept me intact. When I say family, I'm not just talking about my little unit that lives in my household with me, but it extends to my biological extended family, as well as to people who have no blood line to me, but I hold real dear in my circle."

"Our pastor ends every Sunday service with, 'Go home. Take care of your family. Hug your family. Relax with your family.' She constantly promotes family and taking care of each other."

"We had an ecumenical service that in the pulpit and in the congregation we had the Moslem Mosque from the East Side of Cleveland. We had Moslems from Middleburg Heights. We had the Progressive Church and Jews. We also honored policemen and political figures in the community. The Moslems offered their prayers and we offered our prayers. The Jewish Cantor gave their prayer in

the Hebrew language. We had a racially mixed choir dressed in different costumes that gave songs in different languages. I tell you that as that service progressed, I experienced the presence of God. I wanted to jump up out of my seat and go to the altar. I felt the whole congregation lifting it up over all prejudices and barriers. We walked into the presence of God."

"I felt a sense of community and family when my wife decided to celebrate the success of my first book. She planned this elaborate surprise party on my behalf. She contacted some of my old friends, who picked me up and took me on this wild goose chase to visit a friend who was in trouble. We were gone for six hours and I had no idea of what was going on. Weeks in advance she was planning this event. The kids were involved. Friends from the distant past were involved and I knew nothing. When I came to the house, I was shocked, shimmered and surprised by people I had not seen. The fact that my wife would go to this length to show commitment and love made me feel a sense of family. Secondly, to see so many old friends that I hadn't seen in years come and say, 'we want to celebrate this with you, we want to congratulate you, we want to be a part of this moment' was a very meaningful time in my life."

"The community is the way we are connected to each other. We are like one."

Ideal-Type Theme #3: Servant Leadership

The *Ideal Organization* of the Future involves honoring God in all that we do by serving others. The leadership recognizes that we are all created in the image of God and that each created being has a worth and a wealth of potential that is waiting to be unleashed.

Leadership further recognizes that they are stewards of people, a precious treasure of God's and God has entrusted them to nurture and to invest their development.

People have become leadership's highest priority. Leaders within the ideal organization focus on serving others by listening, validating, aligning, training, motivating, inspiring and developing others to be more effective on the job, at home and in their community, to be more productive in their work, and to simply be better people from the inside out.

Through the process of leaders modeling the way, a transformation and a transference takes place where serving others becomes a way of life for everyone within the organization. New leaders within the organization emerge. People then become givers and not takers, helping others develop to pursue excellence and to become all that God has intended for them to be.

By modeling the way, the servant leader enables others to act and turn challenging opportunities into powerful successes within their organization.

Sample Quotes

"Our service is to people and humanity. We are to enrich lives and empower people particularly women and children. As leaders, we are to invest in humanity and empower them." "A servant-leader should be very sensitive to the needs of other people. In fact, they need to model the attitude, 'you first, I'm second.'"

"When leaders and employees are modeling servant-leadership behav-

iors, it will look like activity happening. There will be continuous learning and community involvement because when people are happy they want to do. The phrase 'I can't' would cease to exist."

"A servant-leader should model a genuine sincere love for humanity, a genuine love and deep concern and care for the spiritual, personal and emotional development of others. A servant-leader must have a tremendous willingness to listen to people. I think that as leaders we have the tendency to preach our vision, talk about our plans, dictate, delegate and empower, without ever taking time to gather input from others, to gather the opinions of others in order to create a felt need of belonging. Leaders should make people feel genuinely significant."

"Servant leadership is understanding that we are serving a higher power. We are all servants because God created mankind to be servants to one another. Jesus said, 'Men will know that you are my disciples by the love you show one to another.' So, I think the ability to be humble and to create a sense of servanthood is a great example of God's love in our lives."

Principles

1. We encourage organizational introspection so that our core purpose remains meaningful and inspirational.

2. We progress toward success through unchanging levels of commitment.

3. We give life and meaning to the human spirit.

4. We produce esteem and confidence in people, which allows them to set goals and take risks.

5. We encourage open communication as means to build honesty and trust.

6. We foster a community/family environment that encourages diversity in order to value and respect the differences in others.

7. We partner with the community to encourage support of community activities and projects by providing funding and time.

8. We respect human dignity and individual competencies.

9. We honor God by serving each other.

10. We develop others to pursue excellence and to become all that God intended them to be.

11. We develop people to be more effective on the job, at home, and in their community.

12. We enable our people to act and turn challenges into powerful successes.

13. We enrich lives and empower people to become leaders.

14. We are stewards, entrusted with the responsibility of nurturing and investing in the development of others.

15. We commit ourselves to fostering an environment where people feel proud, significant, esteemed, confident and unified.

Phase Four, "Destiny," involves delivering on the new images of the future and is sustained by nurturing a collective sense of destiny. It is a time of continuous learning, adjustments and improvisation; all in the service of shared ideals.

Remember:

A future does not arrive uninvited. It is built. Organizations begin in the womb of imagination. And when an organization, as a whole, takes time to give voice to its preferred future state, it is all the more likely to become reality. Put simply, it is easier to do things together when there is a common focus. Proverbs 29:18 says, "Where there is no vision, the people perish…"

Chapter **6**

Dunamis for Women

Dr. Danita Johnson Hughes
Author, The Power Within
President and CEO, Edgewater Systems.
Founder of The Johnson Hughes Group
Marathon Runner and Dynamic Motivational Speaker

Consider:

- As a child, I had exceptionally low self-esteem; I just didn't think much of myself.
- I came from a turbulent and abusive family situation made all the worse by the fact that we lived for a time in abject poverty.
- An unwed, mother as a teenager, I had to complete high school on my own; no cap and gown for me.
- I entered into a bad marriage as a result of the pregnancy. It didn't last long, and by the time I was twenty years old I was a divorced, single, mother of two.
- A series of dead-end, part-time jobs led to a full-time job that I absolutely hated.

- I was chronically late for work, and I had a very bad attitude toward my job and my employers.

Those were the facts of my life.
These are also the facts:

- I am currently the president and chief executive officer of a community mental health center in my hometown of Gary, Indiana. As such, I am one of only three women and, until the summer of 2000, the only African-American who can make that claim in the state.
- I am also president of my own consulting and training firm.
- With two master's degrees already earned, I am working toward my doctorate.
- As an inspirational and motivational speaker, I have made appearances around the country.

A lot of people faced with the same or similar circumstances of my background and upbringing might see themselves as victims. I know I did. I viewed my family situation, my becoming pregnant, the bad marriages, the divorce, and the detested jobs as a series of enemies arrayed against me.

In between that first set of facts and the second, something happened. You see, I had met the enemy: and she was me. Eventually, I was able to do something about this "enemy." Eventually, I was able to get her on my side, working for me.

But it certainly didn't seem that way when I was sixteen years old. This was a period in my life when I was very rebellious and also exceptionally unhappy. I was deeply dissatisfied with my home life and had an absolutely awful relationship with my father. My mother I viewed as being too weak-willed, too dominated by my father, to be of any help. There was no other adult to whom I could turn with these feelings that raged within me.

I was looking for friendship, looking for love. I was looking for the things I was not getting at home, but in a misguided, immature way. I made a lot of mistakes in seeking these things. One of those mistakes was becoming pregnant at sixteen.

My parents were, to say the least, not very happy about this development. They offered me little understanding. They made a painful situation even worse. My mother and father wanted me to get married right away, but this was opposed by the parents of the father of the child that was growing within me. Eventually, the boy and I took it upon ourselves to make the decision regarding marriage. I was in my sixth or seventh month when the ceremony was performed.

I gave birth to a beautiful baby girl.

The divorce, the seemingly inevitable divorce, did not become final until five years and another baby later. But the first of a series of breakdowns in the relationship occurred only six months after the wedding. We would get back together, only to break up again.

Eventually, I was almost completely on my own. The task of rearing the children fell almost entirely to me. My mother helped out some, with occasional baby-sitting, but the father of my children offered practically no assistance at all. This embittered me, but also toughened me in a way. I decided I didn't need him, that I was going to do this on my own. On my own was a tough row to hoe. With the help of public assistance, I was able to rent relatively nice apartments, but these rarely contained very much furniture. I took what jobs I could find, but didn't like them very much. I quickly discovered I was not cut out to be a waitress, but still found myself doing just that on several occasions.

Conversations with my father were an endless series of, "I told you so's." It was the last thing I needed to hear and seemingly the only thing he ever said. When even a modest amount of support from him would have made a major difference in how I felt about my life and myself, he would offer none, could offer none. He was always so very negative.

Once I left home to embark on the ill-fated marriage, I vowed that I was never going back. Keeping that vow was so very difficult, with what felt like the entire weight of the world on my frail shoulders.

I suppose the worst time came for me when I was forced to stay with a girlfriend from high school, Toni. A single parent like me, she was living with her mother in an apartment in East Chicago. I had no other place to stay. There was barely enough money for formula and diapers for the baby. She had a bad rash as a result of wearing a wet diaper for longer than she should have.

One evening I decided to go home, but not to stay. I was going to leave the baby with my mother. I was going to admit I couldn't handle this and leave the problem in my mother's lap and go; I don't know where. I was simply going to drop off the baby.

At the last minute, I changed my mind. I couldn't do it. I never even told my mother what I had been planning to do.

It was awful.

In retrospect, I realize that there was a war going on inside of me, from my childhood through my adolescence and on into my early adult years. It was why I was so angry, why I was such a rebel. Even before I became pregnant, there were such low expectations of me, low expectations of where I would end up in life, that I was wracked with self-doubt. When the baby came along, that just added to the stereotypes I needed to fight against.

But I fought against them.

I did so because a part of me wanted to excel. A voice inside my head demanded that I be successful. Part of me wanted a better life.

Part of me wanted to say to others, "You can't define me by your expectations. You can't define me through your limitations."

I guess that side of me won out.

I became the first member of my immediate family to enroll in college, although I don't recall receiving very much, if any, encouragement to do so.

Although my parents, both of them high-school dropouts, were set on each of their children completing high school, going beyond that was simply not in the cards. In fact, in my neighborhood, someone going to college was so out of the ordinary, I felt uncomfortable talking about it once I had started.

I just kept telling myself, that voice inside my head kept insisting, "This is what you want." I began to feel more and more that in order to be happy in my life I had to determine what it was I wanted and then move toward that goal.

I had to be the one setting the agenda for myself.

It really wasn't that difficult. Not once I had made up my mind that I wanted to go to college. I simply focused everything on making certain I got it done.

That might sound easy to say and difficult to do, but it

wasn't. Not really. Not when I harvested all my energy and channeled it into this specific direction.

I applied for and received financial aid and went through an orientation program at the local campus of Indiana University.

I asked a lot of questions of practically everyone I thought might be of help as I set about becoming a college student. There was a man with whom my mother worked at a psychiatric hospital who was also a college student. I had mom ask him about getting money to pay for an education. He recommended a place right in my hometown of Gary that provided assistance to people in filling out financial aid applications.

Finding out that my application had been successful was an absolutely wonderful feeling, tinged with a little bit of disbelief and no small amount of fear. Orientation was only a month away.

I began to question myself.

Did I belong among college students? After all, I only had a GED. I hadn't gotten to march up and receive my diploma like the rest of my high school classmates. There had been no cap and gown, no procession.

I knew I was ready, but wondered if I was truly ready. I knew I could do this, but wondered if I could really do this.

Even though I was barely twenty-one years old, one of my major fears was that I would show up for classes and be so much older than all the other students. After all, people went to college right out of high school, didn't they?

It turned out that at Indiana University Northwest, when I started in 1974, people started their higher education at a variety of ages. Some of the students were easily twice my age, and I soon became comfortable among my new classmates.

My initial plan only included attending college long enough to get an associate's degree. However, the course work and the classes went so much better and time went by so much faster than I had anticipated that, by the time I had enough credits for an associate of arts, I thought: "Why stop now?"

While a lot of major decisions were behind me at the point when I first enrolled in college, many still loomed, and I was completely unprepared for some of them.
Selecting a major was one.

You see, my entire goal had been to get a college degree. In what area of study, I had no idea.

I had not, up to that point in my life, been exposed to a lot of different careers, and had not been through anything like actual career counseling. My background led me to believe that there were really only two professions to which women could aspire: teaching and nursing. Some distant relatives on my father's side were in the teaching profession and, it seemed to me, that field was more open than many to African Americans.

That might be something to shoot for, I thought.

However, in speaking with a cousin of my father's, Ulysses, who was a teacher, I learned that it was not a good career to choose at that particular time. The cousin did impress upon me that I should go ahead and get my college degree. He told me, and it is so very true, that once I got that degree it was something no one could ever take away from me. It was something I would have with me for the rest of my life.

Nursing, then, seemed the clear choice, but then I recalled how unpleasant my experiences had been working in the same psychiatric hospital as my mother, and that seemed like no choice at all.

In fact, I was undecided about a major until I was almost entering my junior year. Then, by chance, I came into contact with the Dean of Public and Environmental Affairs at Indiana University, Northwest, and it sounded like an interesting area of study. He explained that although Public and Environmental Affairs was its own major, there were many different disciplines within it. I eventually majored in public administration with a concentration in criminal justice, the latter as a result of knowing some people who had worked in the local juvenile justice system.

My father used to call me "stubborn." I prefer to think of myself as directed. I was certainly that when it came to applying myself to my studies. I did almost nothing else. My life was work, classes and then home to study and care for the children. I almost never went out with my friends. I knew that I could not have an active social life and see to the needs of my babies while completing college.

Work and school. That was my life.

I knew that there were better things coming, rewards awaiting me down the road for this dedication and determination. But at the same time, I sort of enjoyed this studious existence. There was sanctuary for me in going home and reading my textbooks, writing my papers. I was beginning to think in different ways and starting to expand my horizons. Just as at one point I had been a young woman whose only goal had been a college degree, now I was someone with a definite major and a specific area of concentration within that major.

By going to summer school every year, I received my bachelor's degree in three and a half years, while maintaining a 3.5 grade point average.

I was absolutely elated. Goal achieved. Mission accomplished.

So many people in my life had told me, directly or indirectly, that I could not do this or that or the other thing. So many people had tried, directly or indirectly, to get me to lower my expectations, that it made this achievement all the more special.

The entire time I was in college, my father kept saying that I would never graduate. As I continued earning credits toward my degree, he then complained that I was not spending enough time with my children. With him it was always something negative.

But I was determined. I saw I was going to do this. I said no one was going to stop me.

Not even myself.

Earning that degree opened a lot of doors for me, and it also did a world of good for my ego.

Degrees of Difference

Flipping burgers.

"You want fries with that?"

As a young woman struggling to make ends meet and raise my children with the kind of jobs I could get with my GED, I ended up flipping my share of burgers and asking that famous question over and over again. These were often the only jobs I could find, the only work for which I appeared to be qualified. And I loathed that kind of work.

As a young woman about to receive a bachelor of arts degree in Public Administration from Indiana University

Northwest, I was offered not one but two full-time positions.

Neither of them involved flipping or fries.

One of these was in the juvenile probation system in my native Lake County, Indiana. It held out the possibility of long-term employment and it fit in nicely with my area of concentration in college, which was Criminal Justice. I would have been a part of a major reform of the entire juvenile justice system in Lake County.

The other position was only a summer job, and it was in Crown Point, Indiana (about 20 miles from my home). The temporary opening was for a supervisor of the Comprehensive Employment and Training Act (CETA) Summer Youth Employment Program. There were no assurances this would be a stepping-stone to anything of a more permanent nature.

I took the job that offered the greater risks, and also the greater challenges, and that has made all the difference.

The job of probation officer had its attractions, over and above being a permanent position. A new juvenile court judge had taken over in Lake County and she was determined to bring reform to a system mired in old ways. Most of the probation officers on the staff when she stepped in had been there for ages. The judge wanted to replace many of them, and she had two reasons. For one thing, she felt younger probation officers would be better able to understand the youthful offenders who would be their clients. For another, most of the existing probation officers had gotten their jobs through political patronage, and few, if any, had college degrees. The new judge wanted to instill greater professionalism in the system, and one of the ways in which she wanted to do this was by hiring people who had a higher level of education than the current staff members.

Three things held me back from leaping at this opportunity to take what I had learned in class and apply it in the field.

One involved a tragedy: Earlier in 1977, the year I graduated, a young female probation officer in Lake County had been murdered. Two young men abducted her outside a neighborhood grocery store. While driving around with her in her car, they found the officer's badge. Realizing they were in even greater trouble than if they had simply kidnapped a civilian, the two panicked. They shot and killed the young woman in an attempt to cover up their crime.

Secondly, serving as a juvenile probation officer would have required me to carry a gun. I was not at all comfortable with that aspect of the job.

Finally, though, I was drawn to the CETA position because of one word in the job description: "supervisor." I would be my own boss. It was a lot of responsibility, but after all, wasn't that why I had gone to college?

There was a definite appeal in the idea of helping young people get started in the world of work through the federal program, and the personnel aspects of the position intrigued me. While at Indiana University Northwest, I had served an internship through the School of Public and Environmental Affairs. This involved work with the job classification system in Lake County government, including writing job descriptions and assigning pay grades.

The CETA Summer Youth Employment Program in Crown Point involved working with employers to develop summer jobs for young people, placing youths in these jobs and then monitoring their progress following placement. I was in charge of the job, a development counselor, who went out to the work sites and met with the potential employers. In addition to keeping tabs on these people, I also worked with the employers to make certain the jobs that were developed under the program met the criteria established by the federal act and that they were properly listed with the state Division of Employment.

I learned a lot, and quickly, about supervising people, relating to them and seeing to it that they got their jobs done. I learned some hard lessons about not becoming too close to the people under my supervision, because of the ways in which others might perceive this.

I somewhat surprised myself by absolutely thriving in this job. The work really bolstered my self-esteem. I finally felt like I was measuring up. I finally had something to offer.

Of course, being offered two good jobs, when there had been a time not so long ago when I could find none, had done a lot for my ego. It made me feel good. I remember saying to myself, "Maybe things are finally looking up for you."

I gained extra confidence in myself not only because I had a choice of jobs, but also by succeeding in the one I decided upon.

I didn't let myself dwell upon the fact that the CETA job was going to end once summer was over. For one thing, the work kept me quite busy. More importantly, my newfound confidence had me convinced that something would come along. I had my degree and would eventually find work that was part of a career path.

Besides, I could always flip burgers. You see, I would have known that it was only going to be temporary, until something better came along—as opposed to being the best I could expect.

I was also able to experience, in that first assignment out in the real world, the ways in which my college education applied.

For example, the language, or perhaps a better term is the jargon, spoken by those in the field of employment was familiar to me and really helped in that first job. I know that sounds like a minor thing, but being knowledgeable about the terms used helped make me more confident and increased the confidence others had in me.

Also, some of the classes in management and supervision I had taken had provided me with a good theoretical framework. I was able to go over these theories in my mind as I dealt with the people I supervised, finding ways in which, on an individual basis, they could be put into practice.

I am the kind of person who asks a lot of questions, particularly when I feel uncertain or need some direction. I have been fortunate enough throughout my life to latch on to certain people willing to act as mentors, who provide advice and guidance on how to handle certain situations. I don't know everything. I don't pretend to know everything. Being aware of this, I am able to seek out those who have worthwhile advice, and to listen to them.

As my time with CETA was drawing to a close, I spotted an ad in the local paper for an assistant personnel and payroll manager at the Hammond, Indiana Branch of Purdue University. I applied and was lucky enough to get an interview. I did well in the initial interview with the department manager, and subsequently with his boss. In those interviews I stressed my educational background, the fact that I had already begun studying for my masters, taking classes while working in the Summer Youth Employment Program. I pointed out that I had some personnel and labor relations classes under my belt from my undergraduate days, and I emphasized the ways in which my most recent experiences would help in this new position.

The job of assistant personnel and payroll manager involved recruiting potential employees for all but the management and faculty positions on the Calumet Campus, which employed between 600 and 700 people. The Assistant Manager conducted initial screening interviews and then made referrals of qualified candidates to various department heads. Once these people held their own interviews and made the selection of applicants, the Assistant Manager then handled the paperwork involved in processing new employees.

The university officials were impressed with me, with what I had learned in college and what I had done upon graduating. I got the job.

In interviewing prospective candidates, I followed a system already in place for rating people on their presentation, their academic background and their job experiences. Using my own perceptions, I would rate them in comparison with one another. It was challenging initially, because this was all so new to me and I wanted to do a good job. I was very conscious of how much my referrals of potential employees reflected upon me, how good my judgment was and the quality of my decision making. Always, in the back of my mind, I was aware of the need to refer the best candidates, because it was on this basis that my own job performance would be evaluated.

I did fairly well in this assignment, with one memorable exception. There was one gentleman who kept coming in and coming in to apply for jobs in the maintenance department. He had a very spotty employment record, frequently leaving previous positions after only a month or two. Often these were under less than favorable circumstances— nothing outrageous, but nothing that reflected too well on him as a worker, either. Nonetheless, he kept coming in and coming in. I was impressed with his persistence, and finally passed his name along to one of the department heads. That manager complained to my boss who came to me and asked why I had done what I had done. I explained that the man seemed to sincerely want to work for us, and that he had been so persistent.

I came to realize it had been a bad decision on my part, that persistence is only part of the equation and that other factors must be weighed. I learned from that experience.

I remained in that position for about two years, during which I completed my first master's degree at Indiana University, Northwest. By the time the two years were nearly up, I began to get a little bored with the job. The tasks that had been so challenging at first had become routine. I felt a need for new challenges and began looking for another job.

I saw an ad in the paper for an opening at the Tri-City Community Mental Health Center in East Chicago. It was for a personnel director. I decided to take a chance and applied for the position. I didn't hear anything for a while, but I kept calling to follow up on my application. The secretary to the Director came to recognize my voice. She assured me my application had been received. These things take time, she said.

Time passed and I did indeed get called for an interview with the Director. We connected right away. I was only twenty-five at the time, and he was no more than five or six years older, so we were close in age. We talked about my experiences, what I wanted to do with my life, the kind of background from which I had come. Although I did not meet each and every qualification listed for the opening, he decided to take a chance on hiring me.

Also, he was able to pay me less than someone with more experience—something I found out later on.

Tri-City Community Mental Health Center had not previously had a personnel director. In my new position, I had to put the entire system together from the ground up.

I was more than a little frightened as the enormity of my new assignment became apparent. All the newfound confidence deserted me in the face of such a daunting task. Was I really up to this?

In fact, I was so uncertain of myself that I started working at the Tri-City Community Mental Health Center while on temporary leave from Purdue to recover from minor surgery. It was something I probably should not have done, but I desperately felt the need for that crutch, to be able to fall back on something I did know in the event of falling flat on my face in the new job. There was no one to tell me how to do things. I had to learn entirely on my own.

My new boss was very supportive of me, and I needed every bit of that support. It was an awesome responsibility. The other department heads viewed me as a resource and would bring their personnel concerns to me. I had to provide consultations with them while at the same time trying to set up my own department.

A difficult situation was made all the worse because some of the duties I was taking over had been handled by a woman on the clerical staff. The Director felt that all the existing and coming regulations regarding personnel required a greater degree of professionalism, but many on the staff at the center had a rapport with the woman. They were friends with her and resented me at first. I was someone who was going to come in and disrupt a comfortable situation. Some of my co-workers were not very cooperative at the outset.

After a time, I began to ease into the routine of my new job and to become more familiar with what was required of me. It helped that I had been given an assistant who had been at the center for quite a while.

My personality also helped. I am not, to put it bluntly, someone willing to take a lot of crap from people. I stood up to some of those who made my tasks even more difficult, in particular an assistant director who didn't much care for me. We butted heads frequently. She often complained to our boss that I was not doing my job correctly, but I stood up for myself. My habit of asking a lot of questions helped. Whenever I lacked clear direction, I wasn't shy about asking for it.

At one point, as a result of this assistant director refusing to be pleased with a report I had done, my boss came into my office and we got into a shouting match. He began yelling at me in front of my assistant and with the door to the office open, too.

I yelled right back, because the complaints about my report were unreasonable ones.

After he had stormed out, I told my assistant, "Well, I guess I'll be looking for another job." But the next day, the Director acted as if nothing had occurred between us. Our relationship was unchanged as a result of the argument. It turned out that our relationship was such that we could truly tell one another how we felt, even when this might involve a little shouting.

After I had been at Tri-City Community Mental Health Center for about four and a half years, the center acquired a nursing home. At about the same time, I learned of a job opening at the Gary Community Mental Health Center, in my hometown. It involved the exact same duties and same pay as I was receiving at Tri-City. I applied for the position and was accepted.

When I told my boss this, he was very upset and tried to talk me out of it, but he knew that I was getting antsy in my current job, that I wanted to stretch, to do something different. A big going-away party was thrown for me at a nearby restaurant on a Friday. At the party, my boss came up to me and suggested strongly that I didn't really want to take the new job. What would I think, he asked, about going to work at the nursing home Tri-City had acquired? I would learn new things, he pointed out. I would be involved in hiring or rehiring the entire staff. It would be an entirely different business and a different environment. There were intriguing aspects to the proposal, but I was due to start my job at Gary Community Mental Health on Monday. Let me think about it, I told him.

My boss called me over the weekend and asked if I had thought about it. He then asked me to think about a raise of $10,000 a year if I took the nursing home assignment.

I had one of the worst weekends of my entire life. I couldn't sleep. Part of it was anger at my boss. It was so unfair of him to wait until the eve of my departure to make this offer. I mean, at my going-away party?

On Monday I started at my new job in Gary, but sat down with the Director almost immediately and told her of the opportunity to remain with Tri-City. I told her I wanted to be honest with her and that I was seriously considering the offer.

"We really need you here," she said. "We really need you to straighten out our personnel department."

Here was another guilt trip.

I decided to stay at least a week, take that amount of time to figure out what was best for me. In that period, I began to see that I had stepped into a very troubled situation. Gary Community Mental Health was badly disorganized, in part due to interference and "micro-managing" by members of the Board of directors. I told my new boss at the end of that first week that things were not working out. I called my old boss and said I wanted to come back. I also told him that while I would be returning all the presents from my going-away party, there were still bound to be some bad feelings about this. "Let me worry about that," he said.

I became the Assistant Administrator of the nursing home, with far more responsibility than personnel. In fact, much of the day-to-day operation of the facility soon fell to me.

Since that was the case, I decided to get my license as a nursing home administrator. The process required six months, during which time I began to get a dimmer and dimmer view of what running nursing homes entailed. At about the time this disillusionment began to set in, my position at the nursing home was eliminated.

I needed a job, even if it was flipping burgers.

I updated my resume, and one of the places to which I sent it was Gary Community Mental Health Center. To my astonishment, I was offered the job of quality assurance coordinator. Once again I was faced with doing something I had never done before in my life, but officials at the center must have felt I was qualified for the position. I took the job and then began to figure out what it required, what the Director of the center wanted from the Quality Assurance Coordinator. I met with others in the same or similar positions at other facilities and viewed the systems they had in place.

Naturally, I asked a lot of questions.

After a time, the Executive Director of the center instituted a complete restructuring of the organization. As a result, I became Director of Administration, a position I would hold for the next five years.

I didn't always see eye-to-eye with my direct supervisor. He was, in addition to being my boss, also a state representative, and spent months at a time in the state capital. He seemed to pay more attention to his General Assembly duties, but at the same time was unwilling to give up some of his decision-making authority. I began to realize he was a rather insecure individual. This was my first experience in which I learned nothing positive from my boss. At board meetings, he frequently deferred to me in responding to questions. I was doing an awful lot of work for which I was getting neither credit nor recognition.

I decided to leave.

One of the board members, Sheridan Powell, with whom I had developed a good working relationship, was also on the board of directors of a nursing home. I had vowed not to return to that field, because it can be so thankless and difficult and it is so heavily regulated. Nevertheless, I listened when he told me how greatly troubled this nursing home was. He pointed out that I could hardly make the organization any worse, that practically anything I did would be an improvement.

Also, and this probably tipped me in favor of listening to him, the board member told me it was finally time I assumed the top position of an organization. It might help me in the long run, he said, and would certainly look good on my resume. Who knows, the man said, I might one day return to Gary Community Health as the overall administrator.

With some reluctance, I accepted the nursing home position, but only on a one-year contract. Although great strides were made in improving the operation of the facility, a politically motivated decision eventually led to the closing of the home. I was invited to stay on during the closing, but, as luck would have it, I didn't need to do so. Shortly before my one-year contract was up, I had hired a young man as marketing director for the nursing home. He came to us with a nursing home background in the for-profit sector. When the writing was on the wall in terms of our facility going out of operation, he turned to his previous employer for a job. In the course of his being hired back, I was introduced to some executives with the national firm. They were impressed with the way the nursing home was being run. "How about," they asked, "coming to work for us?"

It seemed like a blessing out of the blue, but the job they had in mind was in Terre Haute, Indiana. I had never really left Gary for any extended period of time, and found myself filled with uncertainty at the prospect.

I had been dating my current husband, Chuck, for nearly five years. Although it was a good relationship, we had no plans to become engaged. In talking with him about what I should do, he commented that for someone facing the prospect of being unemployed I seemed remarkably unconcerned.

And I was. I knew I could find another job.

I could at least flip burgers.

The time came when I had to make a decision. My facility was being closed. I could not afford to sit around and wallow in self-pity. I decided to see this as an opportunity.

I met my future husband for lunch to inform him of my decision. I had found a new job, I said.

"Where?" he asked. "In Atlanta?"

No, I told him. It was in Terre Haute, only two and a half hours away. We could continue to see one another on weekends. This was not an opportunity which I could afford to pass up. The salary was good. My moving expenses would be paid. The for-profit corporation was a leader in the field.

He accepted my decision, but I could tell he was less than thrilled.

The next day he came by to take me to a movie. On the way, he said he wanted to stop at a jewelry store where my sister worked to drop off some watches to be repaired. My sister waited on us. She asked what brought us to the store.

"Actually," Chuck said, "we're here to get an engagement ring."

He had been married before, back when he was in college. He appeared to be one of those men who truly enjoyed the single life. I think he was afraid of getting married again. But the prospect of my moving away made a big difference to him. I accepted his proposal on the condition that we set a date for the wedding, and soon. This was not going to be one of those permanent engagements.

On New Year's Eve 1994, we were married in Lake Tahoe.

I worked at the nursing facility in Terre Haute for two years. During my time there, the home received one of the company's most prestigious awards, the "E Award," for our outstanding performance in meeting licensing requirements. The award brought bonuses and incentives for both my employees and myself.

I returned to Gary on the weekends, and spent long hours

on the road every Tuesday afternoon and evening making the 200-mile round trip to take classes for another master's degree, this one from the University of Chicago's School of Social Services Administration. I had decided it was high time to explore the clinical side of the human services field, in particular the area of mental health.

After two years, I grew exceedingly weary of my commute on weekends. I looked for and found a job closer to home, as administrator for a nursing home in Valparaiso.

I was only there six months, before I made another career move.

It wasn't flipping burgers.

In the End: Faith

I am a Christian.

My faith sustains me.

I rely upon it nearly every day of my life.

It is not necessarily popular in this day and age to make such a statement, and to a certain extent, I can understand why. This is because almost as soon as I put down the words, "I am a Christian" and "My faith sustains me," I feel moved to point out that does not mean I am a religious fanatic.

I am constantly amazed at the uses to which some people put the teachings that have provided the spiritual dimension in my life. How they can have listened to the gentle parables I first heard in my youth and then derive from them a message of intolerance is beyond me.

Too many people, it seems to me, wear their faith on their

sleeves. They attempt to exude the attitude of being so very "grounded" in their religious beliefs that these beliefs seem to be literally all there is to their lives.

Religion, to me, should be about inclusion, not exclusion.

I try hard to let people know I am a Christian, but without being overbearing about it. I seek to set an example for others through my actions. I feel as if I am a good person in large part as a result of my faith in God,

My trust in a higher power enables me to continue to strive to be a good person, and to feel blessed in doing so.

Religion is a part of my life.

I have two things, primarily, to thank for this:

1. My mother
2. Movies

Permit me to explain. The foundations for my Christian beliefs began very, very early in my life. For some reason, my mother insisted that my younger sister and I attend church every Sunday. We were the only members of the family of whom this was required. Not even our mother accompanied us.

Nevertheless, every Sunday she got us up, got us dressed and sent us off to the neighborhood church in Gary, Indiana. We walked there on our own, sometimes on very cold winter mornings, to be embraced by the loving warmth of the congregation inside.

About the movies: I do not mean to imply that my belief in God was inspired by The Robe or Ben-Hur or Barabbas or any other Biblical film. Rather, my younger sister and I both loved the movies when we were little and Sunday was the one-day of the week we were permitted by our mother to go to the local theater.

But only if we went to church first.

So we went.

As I got a little older, I began to grow away from the church, as young people often do. I began to think of our weekly walks down the street as a burden, a form of drudgery. It was not something I wanted to do, but something my mother was forcing me to do. I did not understand the value of the lessons I was receiving in church.

By the time I was a teenager and young adult, I had moved away from the church altogether.

Still, looking back through the charm of time and with the clarity of maturity, I can see now that I did learn some very valuable lessons there among the faithful in my neighborhood church.

I did not fall back on these lessons until I started getting a little older and began to realize there were a lot of challenges out there, that lots of things can happen to us in life.

It can be wonderfully comforting to turn to something bigger than just one's self in coping with these challenges. To be able to draw upon the spiritual base I had developed without really realizing it made me feel less alone when times were hard.

Initially, this return to a spiritual foundation was almost purely internal. I drew on my experiences, on the Bible teachings from that small neighborhood church, for the comfort I needed when I felt so very afflicted.

After a time, I began to feel the need to once again return to a formal church setting as a means of both proclaiming and reaffirming my faith. I once again wanted that "connected" feeling that comes with spending time in religious contemplation with others. I did find connection, to that feeling, that concept of oneness that comes from being part of a church.

My move back into formal religion was aided by a realization that my own children needed to start attending church. After all, whether I liked it or not, it was good for me when I was a child. I began to go to church on Sundays as much for them as for myself. I am certain they felt they were being dragged along to something unpleasant, that they would have much rather remained in bed.

But I know it did them some good. I know they learned some basic values, the kinds of things that remain with one all through life. I think, after a time, they began to recognize the worth of spirituality in their lives.

It is easy when times are good to let the spiritual side slide. As the old saying goes, "There are no atheists in foxholes." When the going gets rough, appealing to a higher power, drawing on one's faith and praying for improvement is important. Beseeching God for a turnaround when everything around you seems negative is almost natural.

I feel, however, that it is just as critical to maintain a relationship with God, to work to sustain beliefs, when we reach comfortable stages in our lives. We can readily forget the need to look to a higher power when our worldly needs are being met.

On a daily basis, I think it is important to understand how very much we have to be thankful for, and to give this thanks to Him from whom these blessings flow.

I have had some very challenging times in my life. From these I have learned how to avoid mistakes, and how to profit from the mistakes I did make. From the hard times, I have learned how a person can make changes in his or her life for the better.

In large part, I was able to make these changes in my own life as a result of the values I gathered to me when I was a little girl in that small church.

Further, and I hope my life reflects this, I feel I have learned from those hard times and from those church-taught lessons how to use my experiences to make things better for others, to make them feel they have the ability and the capacity to change themselves for the better.

That is what I have tried to do here.

Determine Your Personal Power Quotient.

Take the self-test on the following pages to determine your own level of personal power. Remember, there are a lot of factors that play into your sense of control and power over your own life. Personal power is ever changing. But it is manageable.

Personal Power Assessment
Self-Test

Answer the questions below as truthfully and honestly as you can. This is a self-test. No one will see your answers but you. Use this assessment to improve your sense of personal power and thus your degree of satisfaction with your life.

Self Awareness	Always	Most of the Time	Sometimes	Never
	4	3	2	1
1. Everything I need to know to be happy is inside of me.				
2. I am responsible for my own happiness.				
3. My feelings and emotions provide me with feedback as to how I am inclined to act or respond to different situations.				
4. I accept responsibility for monitoring and controlling my own emotions.				
5. My past has taught me valuable lessons.				
6. I release all guilt about my past.				
7. I control my thoughts and focus my attention on positive matters.				
8. I am happy for others in their good fortune.				
9. I can state my views without getting angry or upset.				
10. I am guided by my personal beliefs and values in everything that I do.				
Column Total				

Interpersonal Relationships	Always	Most of the Time	Sometimes	Never
	4	3	2	1
1. I feel that I am easy to like.				
2. I develop supportive relationships.				
3. Although I may disagree with another's lifestyle, opinion, or attitude, I seek to understand them rather than pass judgment.				
4. I focus on being a good listener.				
5. I attempt to make sure that I do not deliberately or intentionally harm others by my words or deeds.				
6. I find it easy to tell people I care about them.				
7. I readily and frequently compliment others.				
8. I attract positive caring people into my life.				
9. I avoid negative people and negative relationships.				
10. I practice unconditional forgiveness.				
Column Total				

Resilience	Always	Most of the Time	Sometimes	Never
	4	3	2	1
1. I view challenges as opportunities for positive growth and development.				
2. I consistently challenge myself to do better.				
3. I am persistent. I go after what I want.				
4. I am not easily discouraged. I handle setbacks with ease.				
5. I am willing to take risks to realize my dreams.				
6. I do not worry about things over which I have no control.				
7. Life teaches me valuable lessons each day.				
8. I make an earnest attempt not to blame others for my failures or mistakes.				
9. I anticipate success, but I am not afraid of failures.				
10. I accept criticism with grace.				
Column Total				

Family	Always	Most of the Time	Sometimes	Never
	4	3	2	1
1. My family relationships are close and supportive.				
2. I have a satisfying and intimate relationship with my partner or spouse.				
3. My family is the most important aspect of my life.				
4. I love the members of my family unconditionally.				
5. I treat all of my family members with respect.				
6. I encourage my family members to pursue their dreams.				
7. My family and I enjoy fun time together often.				
8. I guide my family members toward independence.				
9. I am available to members of my family when they need me.				
10. I am observant and aware of my family members difficulties and challenges.				
Column Total				

Service to Others	Always	Most of the Time	Sometimes	Never
	4	3	2	1
1. Serving others is important to me.				
2. I get great personal satisfaction from helping others.				
3. I am a good mentor to others.				
4. I donate my time, money and my experiences to help those in need.				
5. I encourage my family and friends to volunteer or otherwise assist charitable and other worthy causes.				
6. I reach out to others who need help.				
7. When I give of myself, I do so willingly and I don't expect anything in return.				
8. In all that I do, I consider first whether it is fair to all concerned.				
9. When making decisions that affect others, I base my actions on what will do the most good for the most people.				
10. I consistently try to build goodwill.				
Column Total				

Spirituality	Always	Most of the Time	Sometimes	Never
	4	3	2	1
1. Spirituality is an important aspect of my life.				
2. Through my belief in God I believe I can accomplish anything.				
3. I regularly pray for others.				
4. God loves me for who I am, not for what I do.				
5. I am guided and supported in every aspect of my life.				
6. I am centered in peace, truth, and faith.				
7. I believe that I am abundantly blessed.				
8. I have unique gifts that I willingly share with others.				
9. God is my anchor. I am one with God.				
10. I regularly attend worship services in accordance with my faith.				
Column Total				

Personal Satisfaction	Always	Most of the Time	Sometimes	Never
	4	3	2	1
1. I feel that I am in control of my life.				
2. I have short and long-term goals.				
3. I feel comfortable making sacrifices to get what I want.				
4. I have the ability to make powerful choices and I exercise this ability everyday.				
5. I love myself unconditionally.				
6. I am willing to change and grow.				
7. I feel that I am loved and respected by others.				
8. I try not to be jealous of others who have more than me.				
9. I am optimistic about my life.				
10. I am self-reliant in all matters, including money.				
Column Total				
Grand Total of all Columns				

Add the grand total of each of the columns together for your Personal Power Quotient:

Key: Personal Power Quotient:

310-360 Optimal This is ideally where you want to be!

240-309 Dynamic If your score is here, you're doing great! A little more effort and your sense of personal power could transform your life.

100-239	**Emerging**	What steps do you need to take to improve your sense of personal power and control over your life?
0-99	**Dormant**	Wake up! You've got lots of work to do. But don't despair. You've got the Power!

Chapter 7

Dunamis for the Wounded

Dr. Sean Gilmore
Professor at Baldwin-Wallace College
Speech and Communication Department
Author, Speaker and Speech Consultant

I suffered a back injury that left me immobile and in excru-ciating pain. When I think back to that time I still cringe with thoughts of the pain. I was on all kinds of different pain pills, muscle relaxants and blood thinners. The medication was so strong that it burned a whole right through my stomach lining. As a result, I was then given another medication to protect my stomach.

Still the pain continued to be greater than any of the med-ication could treat. To gain any relief from the pain I had to do the following drills: crushed ice was placed in a specially made bag that I would lay my back upon, I then had crushed ice in bags surrounding my neck, shoulders, and the sides of my back, I would be completely iced every hour. I was unable to do this task myself. Since my wife worked and my son was only three at the time, we had to hire someone to help with the icing procedures.

Lost a Sense of Myself

As each day arrived and constant pain persisted, I continually wondered if I would get better. The days turned into weeks and the weeks into months. I was given no positive prognosis from my doctors of when I might get better. They just did not know. I slowly began to slip into a quiet depression.

In terms of leaving the house, I could not except to make visits to the hospital. I remember once looking at the clock watching the time tick by, and wondering if I would ever recover. Each moment in time seemed like a sentence of pain and immobility. Given that I was not able to work and bring money into the household, I started to feel more and more useless and a burden to my family. I had lost a sense of myself.

I started keeping some of my thoughts on audio-tape. Below is one of the statements that I made during this time: "I am now watching the clock. The secondhand is moving so slow. The minute hand and the hour hand are moving even slower. Each minute I am in pain, and every hour seems like a waste of time. I cannot do anything, but lay here in pain on ice. I feel like I am a burden to my family, and I wonder if I will ever get better."

The Love of a Father

Then my dad came to visit for an entire month. My father was a very spiritual person. He educated me on how to meditate in deep prayer. He taught me that to know God is to know love, and to know love is to know God. He taught me this not only through words, but also through his actions and his love. He cared for me in my darkest hour with the love that only a parent can have for his child.

When he left I meditated every day. I worked to remove all thoughts and to just experience the love of God. This form of meditation gave me a greater connection with God, and a sense of peace. I started to once again appreciate the loving relationships I had with my two parents and my sisters. I was in pain and I was immobile, but now I was no longer blind. I began to once again see how fortunate I was to have a loving wife, and a wonderful son. I started to have joy in every family interaction. I started to enjoy spending time with my son, telling him long stories, reading books and playing games. He would call me "the ice man."

I became more patient with my condition. I no longer asked "why me?" This question suggests that I should be above the pain and suffering that many endure around the world. I began to realize that millions of people are homeless, trapped in poverty or suffering far worse than I, and that I should be thankful just to be alive. I had a home, a family and I was finally able to be grateful once more. Through this gratitude, while in excruciating pain, I became more humble.

A Message Came

I started to think not about my own pain, but about all the pain that exists in the world, as well as all the goodness. I meditated. I prayed. Despite the fact that I was bedridden, I wanted to help others. I asked God for an answer and one came. God filled me with love and my family was always in my vision.

My mother had helped start a rape crisis center, in part because her sister was raped. Through my mother I had also witnessed the power of brotherly love and acted by social engagement. Through her actions I learned the importance of civic involvement, because she has always been a community leader.

I also knew the devastating impact of sexual aggression. Through a research project I had interviewed many women and children whose lives have been torn apart by this violation of their body and spirit. I started inviting friends and former students over to discuss this topic. We collaboratively agreed that education was necessary to remove some of the myths and attitudes that support sexual aggression.

I was now filled with a new sense of dedication and purpose. A person does not hug another unless s/he cares for the other. Why should the most intimate act one person can share with another be something that can be taken from someone? We decided together we would do what we could to raise awareness about this horrendous problem.

The Collective Power

As I lay in bed, still on ice, I trained people on how to run a door-to-door campaign. I asked everyone to speak from his or her heart. Then my friends started knocking on doors, passing on valuable information about sexual violence and asking others to join our educational campaign. Every night more people joined our group that we called 'Stop Sexual Assaults.' Soon, we had over 100 members. We also had people with the local rape crisis center helping us with educational workshops, and we continued our face-to-face campaign. Soon our 100 members grew to 200, then to 500, and then to over 1,000 members. These members contributed money or time to the cause. In addition, we had over 10,000 people sign a support statement that they would talk to others about the myths that support sexual aggression.

We also started participating in radio and television talk shows, including a special on ABC's 20/20. In addition, we gave workshops on the topic to churches, schools, and community organizations. During this entire time I was bedridden. The more I focused on this message that came out of the love I have for my family, a love deeply rooted in God's love, the more I forgot about my own pain. My focus was now on what I could do, rather than what I could not. My parents had taught me a quote from Margaret Mead that stated, "Never doubt that a few committed citizens can change the world. Indeed, it is the only thing that ever does." We were now passing a message onto others about how loving people should treat each other as children of God.

Teach the Message

I meditated more, I prayed more, and I worked more. I found a new sense of energy. I hired someone to transcribe for me and I wrote my dissertation on sexual violence. I finished my doctorate while bedridden. I now had several hundred friends that I could talk to about this important topic that has always meant something to my family. As the days went on, I was never alone when I needed or wanted company.

Since that time I have healed from my injury. I now share

my story of how God's love entered my life during a very challenging time and blessed me with a sense of purpose. Now that
I teach full time, I remind all my students that meditation and
prayer are necessary to hear God's calling. Sometimes God
whispers and yet we are unable to hear him because the stress of
our lives prevents us from hearing his message. You cannot listen to your conscience when your mind is full of clutter.
Everyone needs quiet reflective time, and during these periods a
person should ask himself or herself what is truly important in
life.

Students Following Their Visions

Now when I teach I ask students to create their visions so
they might make a positive difference in the world. In one of
my assignments I ask students to initiate or participate in a campaign for whatever cause that deeply moves them. One of my
students, named Matt Ulrich, stated that he was unsure about
what type of mission he should participate in while at college. I
told him to reflect upon any issues that would have meaning to
him and in time the answer would come.

Several years ago, Matt's father passed away from cancer.
One night, when he was sleeping, his father visited him in his
dreams. When Matt awoke he had a clear sense of purpose, a
vision he should make a reality. He knew a family whose dad
was diagnosed with cancer, and because of the medical bills this
family was going into financial debt. Matt and his family went
into action to raise money for this family. He wrote a mission
for the program that had the following statements:

The reason for this fundraiser for Mr. Morelli is to help him and his family. His wife Paula and their three children, Maria, Vincent and Nina, need money for the medical bills that they have incurred during his struggle with cancer...The Morellis are struggling to make ends meet due to the overwhelming amount of medical treatments needed to fight Mr. Morelli's cancer. Because of this tragedy a committee of friends and family has been formed to help make a difference.

Matt and his family and friends created a non-profit organization and raised $10,000 for the Morelli family. Matt stated that through this event he personally learned that he could make a difference, that he could be involved in something that is greater than him.

I find that each student who follows his vision to have a positive influence in the world motivates others to do the same. The power of Dunamis is a loving, contagious power. Once one person is consumed by the loving compassion to help others, the enthusiasm to have a meaningful life spreads to others.

Whether a person raises thousands of dollars for a charity or personally volunteers every week at a soup kitchen, the collective power of Dunamis can be found. Another student of mine, Angela Staley, was also inspired by the ripple effect of community servitude. The following is her story:

Through compassion for my fellow man I have learned more than a textbook could ever teach. For my senior year of college I opted to live in a unique environment. Five women joined together to form a community service living environment where each of us volunteers in an area of interest. In addition to monthly service projects, each Tuesday I travel to *downtown Cleveland to volunteer at a homeless shelter. These excursions are the highlight to my living in the community house. Special bonds have been formed with the other volunteers and the people I help. My perspective has changed; I no longer go there to volunteer. I have been transformed. I go there to socialize and have fun with fellow members of my community. Hanging out and help`ing has fueled my desire to continue to help and aid those in need when and where I can.*

As a result of this desire to continue to help, I organized a 'Soup Dinner' that would not only educate my peers on the issue of hunger and poverty in Cleveland, but would also give much needed funding to the shelter. This dinner needed marketing. I worked with Professor Gilmore and chose to do my portfolio campaign on the soup dinner I was organizing. Through this process I learned how to really market and work on a campaign that was real. The campaign was no longer a hypothetical assignment to be worked on the night before it was due. The campaign was a real life situation that I had a passion to work on. Service learning opens up the heart and the mind. The bonds I have formed with the shelter and the women I live with have taught me patience, kindness, and love for fellow people.

Both Matt's story of raising $10,000 for the Morelli family, and Angie's campaign for the soup dinner inspired other students in this class. Heather Harvey was deeply moved by Matt's vision, and by witnessing his dream become a reality. She, too, began burning with the desire to make a difference.

The 9-11 disaster had just hit America. My students and myself were all devastated. Heather is the daughter of a minister and a very spiritual person. Therefore she chose to participate and promote a prayer gathering in which 6,000 people prayed for the families of the victims. Heather expressed her experience in the following summary:

> I wanted to support something for which I felt very passionate. When trying to decide what I wanted to encourage, I remembered how much of an impact September 11th had on others and myself. After September 11th I had this desire to try and help out. I am planning on going into the ministry and every part of my being wanted to be at "Ground Zero" ministering to people, helping them process what had just happened. I knew that I could not. So I started to think of different ideas and one day at church my pastor announced several other churches from around the area were going to have a national day of prayer. He explained that they would be using the I-X Center and it was open to anyone who wanted to come and pray for our nation, our leaders, the victims and for each other.
>
> I knew that this would be something that I could help promote with passion. I put together a flyer and brochures, and distributed them out throughout the Cleveland area. I even made a web page about the event.

On the day of the event, 6,000 people attended. It was amazing.

> *Different churches came together to worship. There were several different spiritual leaders representing various religions and nationalities. Each group was praying in their own language for the victims and their families.*

*The prayer gathering lasted for about three to four hours.
This event meant so much to me since I believe that it is so
important for people to be in union with one another. I believe
that a vital key for prayer is building community. Seeing so
many people, nationalities and religions coming together as one
body in Christ was an incredible feeling.*

*I had the opportunity to be on the ministry team and I
helped lead the prayer. This was a time when the leaders opened
the meeting up for people to receive prayer. I loved being able to
pray for everyone and to just minister to him or her with love.
Being able to pray for people who were in so much pain and suf
fering gave me so much gratification, and yet was so very sad
dening. However, being able to witness God bring his love and
comfort to these people, and to be able to see their tremendous
pain eased was astounding. The event was inspiring; I loved
being able to help promote something so profound,whic brought
so many people together to pray for our nation. So even though
I could not go to "Ground Zero", I felt that I was able to con
tribute something during a time when our country was in a state
of devastation.*

Another student of mine wrote the following about a community campaign she initiated and implemented after being
inspired by other students in this same class:

*"United we stand, divided we fall." Following the events
of September 11th, 2001, this message has rung true across
America, Ohio and even my small liberal arts college campus,
as individuals converge to renew and strengthen their sense of
faith, hope, love and kinship. As a member of one of Sean's*

classes, I was directed to create, plan, market and carry out a real campaign on an issue or vision I am passionate about. Inspired by my peers' accomplishments, especially Matt's, I drew upon my own spirituality, as well as the motivation and encouragement of others—especially my teacher.

The idea that came to me was to help implement and promote a Community Relations Awards Night, honoring and uniting individuals or organizations who have served our school and the surrounding community through their dedication to diversity and commitment to spirituality. Over a dozen organizations and individuals were recognized for their selfless acts and practices. The performance of one of the honorees, The Voices of Praise Gospel Choir (VOP), intensified the community-oriented atmosphere. As a former VOP member, I enviously watched my friends perform. But with the contagious spirit of the patriotic, soulful songs, every one stood, clapped and even sang along. I felt more a part of a whole at this moment than ever before. I believe everyone in the old gymnasium felt united toward a common good, as the warmth and strength of the choir's inspirational voices filled the room—as well as the hearts of each person present. The program's success was truly a blessing.

Ron Archer, an alumnus and employer of mine, was honored for his spiritually-based motivational speaking and his offering of experiential learning opportunities to students. I feel blessed to have been taken under this "eagle's wing," invited into Ron's home, and embraced as a partner in his grand vision. From my internship as a Conference Coordinator, I learned the keys to successful teamwork, leadership and utilization of authority as part of a cooperative support system, all while achieving personal growth in the collective power of spirit. Our team's meetings neither began nor ended without a group prayer, and we made sure to never lose sight of the governing power behind our mission to help people reach their visions – our spirituality. I feel honored and extremely grateful for the chance to work with such a dynamic, talented speaker and kindred spirit. When I reflect on my work with the Archers, I am reminded of a *Flavia* quote, "Some people come into our lives and quickly go. Some people move our souls to dance. They awaken us to new understanding with the passing whisper of their wisdom. Some people make the sky more beautiful to gaze upon. They stay in our lives for awhile, leave footprints on our hearts, and we are never, ever the same." I consider the Archer team to be some of these special people in my life.

I have now witnessed hundreds of students touched by the power of Dunamis by following their conscience to live God's compassion. Each stone thrown in the pond makes a ripple, and each ripple becomes a wave of loving energy. I have witnessed students raising thousands of dollars for AIDS research, build houses for the homeless, or, through other actions, living the compassionate power of God's love.

Because of the collective power of Dunamis I could not be more energized by Ron and Cynthia Archer. I have been revitalized by how Ron and Cynthia have created in others and in me a new sense of worship, and a sense of destiny and love. I have witnessed first-hand the power these two have in creating in others a contagious desire to find and follow their own visions.

I have been present when Ron gave a presentation on Dunamis. The entire audience was brought to a heart-felt, long-lasting standing ovation. I have talked to my students and other people now working hard with the Archers to make their visions into reality—everyone is filled with new levels of inspiration to follow God's vision.

Every meeting with the Archers is ended with a prayer and a new sense of hope. To have vision is to see the world not as it is, but as it could be. The Archers have a sense of vision of how positive the world could be. That is, if we all prayed for the power of Dunamis to enter our soul and light up our life. To be in the presence of the Archers is to be filled with the loving power of God, is to be inspired to achieve God's vision of brotherly and sisterly love, is to be given hope that a sense of community among people can be obtained. This is the power of the collective Dunamis. This is the power of this book. This is the power of God's vision.

We must all remember that God speaks to us often in a whisper. When we are too busy with our own thoughts, our own lives, our own stress, we often do not listen to the quiet whispers of God's vision. We must all take time to reflect, to meditate, to pray, to be open. God provides each and every one of us with a conscience—we must learn to listen to the messages within us. Each person will serve the world in a different way. Be open to that vision, listen to it, live it. When we find our vision, and share it with others in the spirit of contagious love that God has for all his children, that is the collective power of Dunamis. Remember that Jesus had twelve disciples and those people helped spread the vision of God.

The collective power of Dunamis is the ability to be inspired by others and to inspire others. Pray for a message, and then it will be your time to sing your song, write your poem, or tell your story. That is, follow the vision given to you with enthusiasm and others will join you.

To actually practice the collective powers of Dunamis right now, do the following: whatever words or stories in this book that have inspired you, share with two other people. These two people can then share the inspiration with two others and so on. Through this process we will change the world, two people at a time.

Chapter 8

Dunamis from an International Perspective

Dr. Aldo Fontao,
M.D. and Masters of Divinity
Vice President and
Director of Leadership Development
The Haggai Institute, Maui, Hawaii

I was 35 years old, lying on a hospital bed when I finally committed myself to try to change my life and transform my existence.

I earned my medical degree when I was 23 years old, in Argentina. A few years later, I completed my graduate studies in cardiology and three years later I completed my studies in sports medicine. I was a successful professional involved in the personal care of several Presidents of my nation, I had my own office, a medical Rehabilitation Center and I was teaching at the university. I was, by all accounts, a success. I had a great profession, influence, fame and wealth.

I had a wonderful wife (Marissa), who shares in all my dreams and all my goals. We also had our challenges in life, including the death of two of our children.

After the deaths of our two beautiful children, we began to identify with the sufferings of others and experienced how painful life can be. We realized, no matter how safe you feel in life, no one gets out of life alive. The faith we received from God has been our support and encouragement.

So here am I at age 35 with my surviving 3 children and my wife, trying to endure our loss and our pain even while our lives are at risk. It was a highly stressful year. There I was, with an infection running all around my body, with serious lung, liver and kidney failure, facing death for the very first time and trying to look for answers, explanations. Full of why's and having just a handful of responses, not good enough to give peace to my mind and soul, I felt like the Biblical character Job in the Old Testament, who lost his children and his health. Why was all this happening to me? I was a decent human being. I was a regular church attendee; I led an easygoing kind of life that never produced deep roots, and I had just enough faith to spend a good time on earth. I would say it was an entertaining life.

Today, I'm in charge of instilling leadership skills in thousands of international leaders in every industry and vocation around the world, who are committed to changing the world and changing history. Some people read history, some suffer history and some wonder about history: others actually write it. In fact, we are writing history.

What happened? Why such a change? In less than 20 years, my entire life was turned upside down. I'm now serving my God with all my heart, and all my strength and all my soul; I am no longer casually involved with God; I am personally committed to God.

As a family we decided (with my wife and children) to live in a different country, in a different culture, learning a different language while dedicating our lives to accomplish a major task: producing change in the hearts and minds of world leaders. Transformation and change are the very essence of leadership.

From these wonderful leadership training experiences, the analyzing and coaching of world leaders from Africa, Asia, South America, Australia, Eastern Europe and the Caribbean has helped me to identify the key elements, the core values, and the core beliefs that produces change and advancement. I have learned first hand how the International Leader thinks, acts, leads, communicates and succeeds.

First Core Principle

"All Meaningful and lasting change starts on the inside and works its way outward!"

Exterior, outward changes never produce lasting change. There are two phases to experiencing Dunamis: first, there must be a "breathe in" experience. The inner being must be reached. I do not use the word "heart" in the sense of the organ that beats inside of your chest, the organ to which we usually attribute the feelings. I rather use the term in the Middle Eastern sense of the "inner-most being," the place where convictions and actions are originated. Once that change is produced, the second step is the "breathe out," or the releasing of that power to the outside world in love and peace.

The second step is always a consequence of the first. This is the real nature of true leadership. Leadership is not what you do; leadership is what you become and who you are after the "breathe in".

Without a "breathe in" there can be no Dunamis leadership.

The first time we breathe in, the moment of our birth, we cry. From that moment, we begin to treasure experiences. Some people do not pay attention to these experiences and do not meditate upon them. But these are the necessary impulses that move us in certain directions. We start to explore the paths that lead us to our true destiny in life. When you have a clear idea of where you want to go, people will adhere to it if it is a valid challenge for their lives, because they have had the same kind of "breathe ins" but did not know how to do the "breathe outs". There exists a collective identity of a shared experience. Remember the movie, *Close Encounters of a Third Kind*: each character in the movie had been touched by an extraterrestrial. The encounter with the "ET's" produced an insatiable intrinsic motivation to first create through paintings, sculpture or music what they had "breathed in", what they had experienced. These touched souls lived in different cities, in different countries, but were connected by a common significant supernatural experience. Those who lived with the touched souls could not understand what had happened to their loved ones. They were different, they were changed somehow by the experience; they were focused on finding out why they had been touched in such a deeply meaningful away. They were driven to connect with others who had been similarly touched by the supernatural experience. They were having difficulty with their "breathe outs." The untouched simply could not understand or relate to their life-altering experiences.

Looking for Examples

We can analyze Dunamis leaders like Mahatma Gandhi, Mother Theresa, Nelson Mandela, Pope John Paul III, or even devilish leaders like Pol Pot, Slobodan Milosevic, Adolph Hitler and Joseph Stalin. They do not just appear out of nowhere. These leaders are reacting to their environment. We can agree or disagree with the reaction, but all of them led some degree of change effort, positive or negative. The more we learn about their lives, the more we realize the inner factors that shaped them, the more we realize that they were not born leaders. They developed a vision from a significant emotional experience that forever changed them. For some they chose a path of goodwill; for others they chose a path of bitterness and hate. People who had experienced similar significant emotional experiences aligned themselves with these leaders in order to fulfill a destiny. True leaders have the ability to attract, like a magnet, the voluntary commitment of others in order to achieve a goal beyond their own comfort zone.

The release of Dunamis makes the world move ahead in some direction. The perceived lack of leadership around the world occurs because today's modern leaders are producing only exterior changes: superficial. The fragmentation and the commercializing of Christianity are hindering an integrated "breathe in." There are no answers, no questions, everything is directed to "entertain life." People are lasting, enduring, not living. We are more and more inward-oriented and more and more isolated.

Jesus Christ appeared in this world to offer to humankind a personal relationship with the Father. We have taken what was meant to be a relationship and transformed it into: 1) A Philosophy; 2) A Legalistic Institution; 3) An Ethnocentric

Culture; and 4) A Profitable Commercialized Enterprise.

No wonder Jesus says, in the Book of Revelation, "I stand at the door and knock." Jesus is not addressing non-believers, He is addressing the modern church. He is saying that the church has become so corrupted with worldly pursuits that His original message of a relationship has been lost and forgotten. He is now standing outside the very church that bears His name.

Dunamis is not a power "for me"; it is a power "for we" to be released. It passes through me but the final destination is the world. We are intermediates. We are channels... as long as we are ready to let it be.

Chapter *9*

The Dunamis Institute
Transcendent Leadership Development

This document is the intellectual property of The Dunamis Institute and its founding partners and directors. It contains certain confidential information and may not be reproduced in whole or in part without specific written authorization.

*"But we have this hidden treasure in clay pots, that the Excellency of transcendent power (**Dunamis**) may be of God and not of us. We are hard-pressed on every side, yet not crushed; we are perplexed, but not in despair; persecuted, but not forsaken; struck down, but not destroyed!"*

- The Apostle Paul to the leaders of the Greek City of Corinth (II Corinthians 4:7-8).

Table of Contents: Chapter Nine

Introduction

The events of September 11, 2001 (9-11), demonstrated to the entire world the undeniable value of Dunamis leaders. In the midst of an unprecedented national tragedy, one man, New York Mayor Rudolph Giuliani, was a tower of strength for the people of his city – and indeed the people of our nation. During this trying period, Giuliani – who had long been viewed as a prototypical, autocratic "command and control" manager—was able to tap an inner source of spiritual strength, and the results were astonishing: the hard-boiled Giuliani was revealed to us anew as a feeling, compassionate and soulful leader. His leadership demonstrated a wonderful blend of efficiency and spirit, touching both the mind and the heart. Not only did he bring order out of chaos, he brought hope out of despair.

To get the most out of the populace, organizations of all kinds need visionary leaders who can connect with their people on a spiritual and emotional plane – leading them rather than managing them, inspiring them rather than directing them. In short, today's organizations need Dunamis Leaders.

Just like Mayor Giuliani, the average leader in the 21st Century is facing the three C's...overwhelming complexity, increasing competition and accelerated change. Leaders of spiritual, political and corporate organizations cannot know enough, about enough, fast enough to do enough to keep themselves and their organizations nimble and responsive to the three C's of complexity, change, and competition.

A recent survey by a leadership journal reported that leaders are overwhelmed by the pressures of modern technology, customer demands, work-force diversity and shareholder expectations, all of which produces moral and ethical challenges. The question arises, "Does the end justify the means?"

These leaders revealed that they have more authority, but less employee commitment, more technology, but less human interactions, more leisure items, but less time to enjoy them. They have less time for family, faith and friends. Many have admitted they've lost their way and are living out lives in quiet desperation. Prescriptions for anti-depressants are at an all-time high, while leaders search for transcendent power and the elusive quality of life in the midst of chaos and confusion.

Even ordained clergy are not immune from burn out and emotional collapse. Since the tragedies of 9-11, churches have been swamped with fearful souls searching for answers to the realities of death and life. Cuts in social programs have sent the homeless, unwed teen parents, the poorly educated, the unskilled, the mentally disturbed, the physically sick and the recently paroled running to the church looking for answers, money, job training, literacy, parenting classes, drug treatment and housing. Pastors have the heart and the compassion to help, but, in many cases, they lack the funding, the organizational structures, the staffing, the strategic plans, the leadership skills and the professional development to meet the demands.

Government agencies were never designed to provide all the social and spiritual services that have become entitlements for a generation accustomed to looking to Uncle Sam for life, liberty and happiness. A growing and aging population has needs that run counter to the priorities of their younger tax-paying neighbors, who feel overburdened by an uncertain future as generational caretakers of the very young and the very aged.

A leader's quality of life determines his/her quality of effective service. Pastors, business leaders and civic leaders in our large, poor, urban centers face this reality more than most. Pastors, mayors and business leaders, in cities like Cleveland, Detroit, Atlanta, Houston, Baltimore, Chicago and Los Angeles, are facing mounting demands with limited resources.

How do you feed 5,000 hungry, poor, children with only 2 fish and 5 loaves of bread?

What is The Dunamis Institute?

The Dunamis Institute for Transcendent Leadership in the 21st Century is designed, staffed and organized with mature and successful Christian leaders who are medical doctors, university professors, motivational experts, clergy, organizational development clinicians, athletic coaches and corporate executives, all of whom possess deep spiritual principles that developed through their own Dunamis experiences. These spiritually experienced leaders offer other leaders an opportunity and a place to find their second wind in order to continue the race in leadership, ministry, and service. Empowered and renewed with increased IQ's (information quotient), AQ's (adversity quotient), TQ's (talent quotient), and CQ's (character quotient), the renewed leader can now lead with transcendent power.

Leaders need an opportunity and a place to be refilled with the awesome treasure of transcendent power, strategic planning, appreciative problem solving, revenue enhancement strategies and spiritual renewal; A place where they feel safe to be vulnerable and free to grapple with the realities of being a fragile, earthen clay vase that is constantly being emptied of its contents by a demanding and desperate constituency.

How a leader refills his/her clay vessel determines his long-term potency, and what he refills it with determines whether he has a breakthrough or a breakdown.

Dunamis: Transcendent Leadership Power

What exactly does that mean in today's fast-paced, electronically dominated world? How do leaders rediscover, redefine and realize the power that is available to them to overcome and rise above the challenges of the modern city-state? What's the right balance of work, family, friends, spirituality, health and financial well-being? How can leaders choose among these major demands, given limited time? Are leaders making meaningful contributions to society, or are leaders just so busy that they have confused activity with accomplishment?

What is the Vision of The Dunamis Institute? A Learning Christian Leadership Organization

The Dunamis Institute is a non-profit, faith-based educational entity, serving as both a training organization and as a think tank for examining new ideas and disseminating information within the leadership community, primarily in our large urban centers. The Dunamis Institute is strongly committed to the Gospel of Jesus Christ and his last command to the Apostle Peter, "If you love me, feed my sheep." We are going to focus on feeding the shepherd in business leaders, political, educational, ecclesiastical and social change agents who, in turn, will feed their sheep (or their sphere of influence).

A Network of Transcendent Leaders

The Dunamis Institute is also about people coming together, sometimes in person, sometimes electronically, who are passionate about exploring the potential of Dunamis being unleashed in our urban cities to transform the desert of hopelessness into an oasis of success and progress. The Dunamis Institute is about producing results in the real world, quantifiable and quantitative breakthroughs that will raise the standard of excellence in our inner-cities.

A Process

The workshops, forums and retreats will give leaders the tools and the methodologies to examine their circumstances so they can build and construct new models and systems that offer lasting spiritual and practical improvement. These Christian-based programs will facilitate the exploration of new perspectives and the development of realistic initiatives that empower both the leader and the organization that he/she leads to make greater contributions to communities of which they are apart.

A Christ-Centered Environment

The Dunamis Institute is a spiritually-driven place, with the sole purpose of equipping men and women of faith to fulfill the kingdom command of being witnesses of God's transcendent power in the lives of his people. It is a sanctuary-like setting where intellectual stimulation is interwoven with the natural beauty of Maui's awesome reflective ambiance. The use of nature as a metaphor for life is a thread throughout much of what The Dunamis Institute is all about. People from all walks of life already visit Maui, not just for world-class resorts and recreational facilities, but also for the stimulation and spiritual renewal that the Hawaiian Islands and the people who call it home offer.

In summary, the vision of the Dunamis Institute is to be a healing, networking, learning community that enables leaders to renew their faith, rekindle their passion, revive their commitment to contribute more effectively and more broadly to the feeding and stewarding of the flock that God has placed under their care...whether it be in business, politics, education, sports, church, entertainment, or social service.

As Jesus said, "Let your light so shine before men that they may SEE your good works and glorify your Father which is in Heaven."

Trends

As the work world continues to shrink vertically and grow horizontally, leaders are being asked to do more with less. As the forces of global choices and the epidemic of worldwide quality increase, the leadership span of control is also increasing exponentially. Good management without Dumanis Leadership is the epitome of an organization that looks good, while going nowhere.

Leaders must be able to gain the voluntary commitment of those that they lead because having a title is just not enough. Customers are demanding that organizations delight them with high-speed, super quality and cost competitiveness. As Ken Blanchard would say: "the challenge is to transform customers into raving fans who not only deliver on promises made but also quite often exceed promises made."

At the Dunamis Institute we foresee an emerging "age of potential and purpose" in the business world. We believe that every individual has an innate desire to add value and to be productive based on her or his unique purpose, passion and calling. We believe that people are created by divine design to shine for the Glory of God. Consequently, the true challenge for today's leaders is whether their organizations can thrive and survive without maximizing the innate creative potential of each team member.

Before you can turn your customers into raving fans you must first turn your employees into raving fans. Enthusiastic employees at the point of customer contact are very contagious.

To meet the demand of the new millennium, leaders are asking themselves: "How can we ignite the hearts, minds and passions of our people to achieve peak performance under peak pressure?"

The demands of a growth-oriented career leave precious little time for the other important matters of a leader's life. These pressures of peak performance often result in lives that are precariously out-of-balance, causing ill health, marital discord, family alienation and general breakdown and burn-out.

Set against these demands and stresses are the desires among today's leaders to live fuller, longer, more meaningful lives, while becoming more involved in contributing to the cause of Christ. Who takes care of the leader, who takes care of the sheep? Who encourages the leader when despair arrives; wearing battle fatigues? Where does the leader go to retool both spiritually and intellectually? Many leader retreat centers focus on the profession, but not on the person. Leaders are human beings, not human doings.

Programs

By challenging leaders to look deeper into their lives, the diverse programs offered by The Dunamis Institute will address these and other questions critical to leadership effectiveness. The Dunamis Institute will launch an international forum, bringing together Christian thought leaders in every significant discipline to explore practical approaches for designing the curriculum to help leaders develop and unleash transcendent power in their world of influence. The institute will also offer weeklong retreats and conferences for individuals and groups in order to provide the tools, strategies, and life management skills that will provide them with the ability to live a more balanced, inspired and meaningful life.

The Dunamis Institute's first programs will be offered in December of 2003 and will continue to evolve over the next ten to fifteen years. This concept paper outlines the vision for The Dunamis Institute, with the goal of receiving input from leaders in churches, businesses, social services, agencies and potential financial supporters.

Participating in the development of this learning organization by becoming a founding contributor will provide a unique opportunity to leave an imprint in lives of leaders for the cause of Christ. If this concept captures your interest and you are willing to help propel it into reality, then we would like to begin a dialogue with you.

Setting of The Dunamis Institute

The Dunamis Institute is located on the beautiful island of Maui, Hawaii, in the warm, soothing city of Kihei. The island of Maui is a very spiritual place where life is slow, reflective and precious. There are six microclimates and breathtaking vistas that heal the mind and invigorate the soul.

The Haggai Institute, which prepares third world leaders for global evangelism, is also located there due to the special power that radiates from the island, the ocean and the people. Maui is 3,000 miles from the nearest continent, and when ocean breezes massage your face, the wind has been purified through 3,000 miles of travel through the open sea. The songs of humpback whales serenade the night and tropical birds sing with the dawning of each new day.

Maui is the closest place to the original Garden of Eden on Earth. On the big island of Hawaii, God is still at work creating new land and new life out of fresh lava flows. This "genesis effect" of new beginnings impacts the special ambiance that is the Aloha spirit; it forever changes people's perspectives of what is really temporal and what is truly eternal and meaningful. Maui is a place where leaders will discover their own new beginnings with the help of the staff at the Dunamis Institute.

Setting is key to a successful program. When people are brought together to contemplate such an important matter as transcendent leadership power for the 21st century, creating the right environment becomes more critical than simply providing a nice location. The environment must be provocative and inspiring, yet professional. It should foster deep reflection, but be accessible; it should provide opportunities to contemplate God's creation, while facilitating a wide variety of outdoor activities, and the ideal atmosphere must be comfortable, yet challenging—all of which the island of Maui provides.

Founding Directors

The founding directors are establishing a new non-profit 501(c)3 organization under the Dunamis Institute name. The Dunamis Institute will be formed by several individuals and organizations based in Maui and Ohio.

Day-to-day management will be handled by a select group of Christian leaders headed by Ron Archer, Cynthia Archer, Dr. Danita Johnson Hughes, Dr. Sean Gilmore and more to be named later. A Board of Elders will govern the affairs of The Dunamis Institute.

Additionally, The Dunamis Institute will establish a Board of Fellows—distinguished thought leaders and scholars who will contribute to the intellectual direction of the organization and its activities. Separately, a Board of Advisors will be created to ensure that a broad-based cross section of ideas and expertise are available as The Dunamis Institute evolves.

Principal sources of revenues for the Dunamis Institute will be participant fees and sponsorship support from corporate strategic partners, foundations and President George W. Bush's faith-based initiatives.

Next Steps

At this juncture, the founding directors will convene and develop a comprehensive business plan that will articulate the Dunamis Institute's concept in considerable detail. This plan will include financial projections, an organizational structure, specific program descriptions, both a market and a competitive analysis and personal profiles of the key players.

For information on how to get involved call 1-800-3-ARCHER or email at **Archer@Archerassociates.com**

Chapter *10*

Today is a New Day

Teresa Bower
Manager of Organizational Development, BNSF

Today is your day to take control of your life - take control
of certain outcomes, choices, decisions, to discover the possibilities hidden within you, and the opportunities that surround you.

I want to share my story with you with the intent to show
you that you are not alone. Obstacles are in front of each of us;
it's how we choose to react to those obstacles that make our life
what it is. Whether it is your weight, your career, or your personal life, you have the power - you own it - it's within each of
us to discover.

I dedicate this writing to each of you. You can be who you
want to be, live how you want to live; it's all about you! We are
each important; there is a reason you are here. It is imperative
you treat the people whose paths you cross with kindness and
without judgment. Learn from your experiences, take each one
whether it is positive or negative and recognize that this opportunity is allowing you to grow as a human being. Share those

experiences with others. Remember the saying, "Knowledge Is Power"? It is extremely powerful, so share it!

Live each day, as it was your last! Who would your last phone call be to? Does that person know how you feel? Do they know where they stand with you? Have you told them? What if. . .just what if?

Remember. . .Life is short. . .Passion prevails. . And it's always about the PEOPLE! Enjoy!

Enjoy!

Teresa

My New Day

My new day began, February 1, 1997, the day my daughter Sydney was born. She had big blue eyes, blonde hair, a killer smile, and never cried. While she weighed in at 8lbs and a few ounces, my weight had soared to 268 pounds. The number on the scales, 268, were more than numbers, there was so much more behind those three numbers and how I got there. I was at the end of my marriage to Roy for the second time. I had three other children who needed their Mom to not only take care of them, but also to feed, nurture, comfort, drive to and from soccer, and take to the Doctor or Dentist when needed. While I was taking care of the most important people in my life, I neglected the person that should have been at the top of that list . . .me. Shortly, before Sydney was born we finally had our family portrait taken. I had put this one off for years, I always had weight to lose and never wanted the camera to reflect what I deep down already knew, I was severely obese. I would much rather say I was just a little over weight, but I saw one of my Doctor's write ups after a car accident I had that year. The written word on my chart, **'obese'**, stuck out and slapped me in the face. I thought I hid it very well! The big black shirts, black stretch pants, heavy makeup, and the big Texas hair were my cover! Surely my cover couldn't be blown; no one would realize how heavy I really was? Not so, while there was no fooling the Doctor, the camera was screaming, "Hey lady, nice smile - what's up with the triple chin?" So, there it was, the picture, I thought that the denim theme for all of us was a nice touch, definitely showing my fashion sense, after all I was a buyer for a major department store! The proof was in front of me; my cover had been blown. I WAS severely obese.

I couldn't play with my children without becoming tired, when I walked in the Texas heat my legs rubbed raw - causing bleeding thighs. I had to apply baby powder with cornstarch to ease the pain. Sitting down was no problem; it was the getting up that was my struggle! What happened? How did I let myself get this way? Whose fault is it? My parents? Did they force-feed me Dominoes Pizza and Chocolate Chip Cookie Dough ice cream? Unfortunately, I had no one to blame but myself. The years of bad food choices, lack of exercise, and a negative self-image was the road that led to 268.

February 1, 1997 was my day, Sydney was born! I had to take control of my life; I had to exercise my very underused willpower. It was a very slow start. I began with the end in mind. I visualized myself at the size I knew was healthy for me, and took my first walk around the block with my kids not long after we came home from the hospital. I had to allow myself enough time so I wouldn't miss my Oprah on TV! With my first walk under my belt, I was ready for the next one, and then the next until I was ready for the TREADMILL!

I'll never forget that first day on the treadmill. The setup in the gym was great! The row of treadmills faced out towards the windows, and there were mirrors in the back of the gym. Many, many mirrors! That's when I caught a glimpse of her, a large woman in the back of the gym. She had black hair, the same shirt on as I did, walking the same pace as I was, it was her back I could see, I was trying to get a look at her face, and when I moved she moved at exactly the same time just the opposite direction. No way . . . the lady, the large lady, she was me! I wanted to run, not on the treadmill, run away, as far away from that gym as I could. Again, how did I let this happen? Thank the big guy up above, I did not run, I kept my visual in mind of what life would be like when I was at my healthy size, and kept thinking of the movie Rocky with the 'Eye Of The Tiger' theme song blaring!

I walked for four years (no not straight!), and then began to run at the end of the fourth year and continue into my fifth year of healthy living. I ran my first 5k, then 5 miles, then my first 10k! As of this writing I am within "NINE" pounds of my weight goal of 155 pounds. Yes, as of today, May 2, 2002, I weigh 164 pounds! I have shed over 100 pounds of layers to find the person that I have always been, just not viewable to everyone else! It has taken 37 years to get to where I am today, and 5 of those years to realize I have the power, I make the choices, I own my free will! I say yes to life, to living life - every second with the passion of believing it could be my last! It was the good and bad food choices I made that got me here, it was the positive and negative attitudes that pushed me over the obstacles, I believed I could do it, I believe I can do it! I choose to live a healthy, happy, and long life! You can too!

Following are five key reminders that have helped me along the way:

Visualize your goal(s)!
> **1. Don't be so hard on yourself - forgive yourself!**
> **2. Celebrate Everything! Here, here to your successes and your obstacles!**
> **3. Surround yourself with positive energy/people!**

And most importantly . . .

> **4. BELIEVE! Believe in yourself!**

Let the journey begin!

Your friend!
Teresa

Visualize Your Goal

Shut your eyes and think about what it is you really want. Who it is you really want to be? How do you see yourself? Think about what you see when you do shut your eyes. Do you see yourself playing with your children? Walking down the street?

Living healthy? First, you must be true to yourself, be realistic. Take a look on any grocery store magazine rack. On the front page you will see the word "WEIGHT" in bold letters on almost every magazine. Let's face it, Weight loss sells. Now take a look at who is on the cover. Amazing isn't it? Unless it's a copy of Rosie, I adore Rosie; you will see a beautiful, thin model on the same cover of the same magazine! What message are you picking up? Better yet, what message are we sending our children? Think about it; is an individual's appearance the means of acceptance by society? Do we treat people differently based on their height, weight, and skin color? You bet we do! When I weighed in at 268 the salespeople at several stores were in NO rush to assist me.

I'd be lying to you if I said I boycotted those magazines. I buy almost every issue. I thought for sure that I would find the *'weight loss cure'* within the pages of these magazines. I have to say I am an avid reader of the 'health' magazines. You will still see the thin, beautiful person on the front. Just look past the cover and you will be able to gather some excellent information on not just weight loss, but healthy eating, and healthy exercise habits. This is one of the *secrets* to my success. I was motivated by the weight loss stories featured in the health magazines every month. There are *'real'* people, with *'real'* problems - like me! It was fascinating to see how they lost weight, and what they did to do it! It was here that I discovered what worked well for some people. Every person's success story began with the end in mind (visualize), they drank plenty of water (8 - 8 oz. glasses a day to be exact!), and exercise played a key role, not only each person's weight loss, but in creating a healthy frame of mind!

So, the true adventure began! Once I had my mind made

up there was no stopping me! Yes, I have had several setbacks. My first setback was the holiday involving a lot of candy! YOU know which one I'm talking about! You know two treats for the kids and one for me! The first seventy-six pounds had taken me about a year and a half to lose I walked thirty minutes a day, drank my water and ate several small healthy meals throughout the day. The first setback brought back twenty pounds. The next setback was a two for one deal! I lived through another divorce with Roy and received a promotion at my job! While the Divorce was a heartbreaker - the Promotion was a distraction.

The distraction came in the form of many long hours, less focus on eating and drinking, and almost no walking! Before I knew it my weight crept back up to 210! I experienced an incredible loss in energy. I was always tired, irritable, and my everyday spark had fizzled.

When I let go of my spark, I also let several important relationships in my life fizzle. My reaction to an exciting story or event that happened to one of my children was less exciting than grocery shopping! They could sense it, I knew it, but chose to be sparkless. Until the day we lost my Aunt Betty to cancer. My Aunt Betty, mother to three boys, Michael, Thomas, and David, (all grown) wife to Robert, sister to my Mom, Fran, sister to my Aunt Linda, and daughter to my Grandma, Eva had lost her fight for life right in front of our very eyes. I've never known or seen anyone in hospice care. Little did I know that once hospice steps in, the next visit is to the funeral home. Knowing how much she wanted to live, seeing the last tear fall from her face, I knew I had to live my life the way it should be lived, as if it were the very last day of my life! It sometimes takes a life-altering event such as this for us to get back on track. I could have gone on existing everyday as I did, blaming my current problems for what happened in my past, but it was time to step up to the plate and hit a homerun. I have control over this life, and I better start taking action, NOW!

I had previously put off joining Weight Watchers during the year I had no spark, until I finally decided to give it another try!

My first weigh-in was 210 pounds; that was two years ago. As mentioned earlier I weighed in at 164 pounds. My weigh-in today found me at 166.8. That's a gain of 2.8! I still experience the same setbacks that we all do! I know that I will reach my goal! Small setbacks are ok! What a perfect lead into the next topic! "Don't be so hard on yourself - forgive yourself".

Don't be so hard on yourself - forgive yourself

I wish I could tell you that losing weight was easy. It was and is something that I consciously think about everyday, almost every hour. I had to make a choice to "live healthy" rather than "diet". The word diet for me meant certain failure. Diet meant sacrifice and hunger! My weight issues began in high school. My first real job was with McDonalds. The food choices at McDonalds weren't what they are now. There were no salads or grilled foods to choose from. The year was 1980 - fat grams, carbohydrates, and proteins weren't front-page news! My 'four food groups' consisted of Big Macs, French fries, Chocolate Shakes, and hot fudge sundaes with extra hot fudge and extra nuts! Do you know how incredible French fries are in tartar sauce?

To understand my situation even further I need to reveal something to you that is extremely painful, and at the same time very uncomfortable to discuss. However, I want to reach out and help each of you, and to do so, I must be honest with you and with me. I want to extend a hand to those of you who may be in, or have been in the same situation I was, and to know that there is hope for you. Here goes . . . Someone close to me took advantage of me for about two of my high school years. I can't believe I'm sharing this with you, please understand that I have forgiven this person. I may never forget what happened, but as GOD is my witness, and we've had many conversations about this, I forgive this person. The impact these events have had on my life are phenomenal. For years I chose to hide behind the extra layers of pounds so that I wouldn't bring any attention to me. I always convinced myself that the next diet would find the true Teresa at the core of my being. Typically I would come within 25 pounds of my goal. Then, people would begin to comment on my appearance, and how good they thought I was looking. The attention was short-term, I was actually afraid of how I should react to the comments, and I just wasn't sure how to handle the attention.

Forgiveness is something we are not inclined to do as much as we should. When I said that these events had a phenomenal impact on my life - they did. After I was finally able to bring forgiveness into my heart, I moved forward with my life. I had been blaming so many people for what had happened to me! I stepped back and took a good long look at what had happened and was able to understand that the outcome actually made me the person I am today! I was able to understand what power I had! I realized that I had the power to learn from what had happened and could either choose to be miserable for the rest of my life or to move forward and live life to the fullest! I choose to live life to the fullest!

Back to forgiving yourself . . . You know what? You can have your cake and eat it too! I do! I make daily adjustments! As a matter of fact, it is 9:45pm and I'm eating strawberry short-cake! Yes, I ran over 4 miles today, drank my 8 glasses of water, and I'll bump up my protein intake tomorrow - still I am eating my cake, loving it, AND wearing size 6 shorts! Isn't life grand!

With each day a new challenge is certain to approach you.

Unfortunately you will not be able to predict what challenges or circumstances you will be faced with, keep in mind that you do control how you react to these obstacles! One such obstacle for me has been joining my friends for lunch. Lunch is always a great time to socialize and catch up on peoples lives. It's where the crowd chooses to go to lunch that I've found at times to be frustrating. Most restaurants have many healthy food options for you to choose from, some do not. In order to make this a positive situation I'll order the healthiest food choice available. Sometimes I may have brought a healthy food choice and will eat it at the restaurant. Other times I'll drink extra water before my meal arrives and modify the menu item I order - the grilled chicken without the mushroom sauce, etc. You get the picture, remember it's within your power to make the choice you want. If you do want to enjoy a lunch out, do it! I know that the days I sway from my food plan will add to length of time for me to reach my ultimate goal. So, my thought is - is it worth another day? You choose.

It is imperative that when you slip, you pick yourself back up! It's OK! We can be so hard on ourselves! There is no reason to make yourself feel guilty about enjoying something you choose to eat! One piece of advice: if you are going to eat it,

ENJOY IT! You don't have to throw in the towel just because you ate a brownie or had the root beer float (A & W still has the best ones!) I'll never forget the wedding reception of two close friends, Debbie & Troy and the amount of food that was available! I was going to be strong until the freshly baked bread was placed in front of me, with the creamy whipped butter! I decided to eat as healthy as I could, but I also chose to eat that fresh baked bread! At the end of the day I told myself, "You should go ahead and write down everything you ate just to show yourself the choices made that day!" I did! Not only did I go over the amount I would typically eat, I ate enough for three days! The difference in me that day versus year's prior, is that previously to making the jump on my new way of living I would have felt guilty and just given up! Instead, I slipped and was back on the program the next day! I had to recognize that this was a celebration that I chose to celebrate!

Celebrate Everything! Here here to your successes and your obstacles!

I wake up everyday thankful for another day to Celebrate Life! I always have in mind, Life is short, Passion prevails, and it's always about the people! Life IS short and so very precious. We forget that each day, each moment is soon to be in the past.

It's what you make of every moment that counts! I choose to live each day celebrating. I celebrate being called Mommy by my children. I celebrate that I have the ability to walk, run, laugh, cry, and love! Tomorrow could come with a different approach, a different way of life. So, taking for granted what

GOD gave me is something I refuse to do! Free will is a powerful thing! We all have free will. The cost is nothing! We have the ability to make choices, whether they are deemed right or wrong we have the ability to make these choices. Think about some of the choices in your life that were difficult or what you think may have been the wrong choice. I'll bet there was a lesson learned from each experience. I married Roy twice. I learned so much about myself both times! If I had not married Roy the second time Brandon wouldn't have Chris, Ashley or Sydney to call family! I celebrate this! I celebrate the fact that Roy found an incredible Wife and Co-Mother to my children, Kier. Kier is the piece of the puzzle my family was missing. She is an amazing human being. She is understanding, compassionate, beautiful, intelligent, and most of all, my friend. I consider myself lucky to be able to count her as family. It DOES take a village to raise a child!

The true success of my journey is the food choices that I make each day. I begin each day with protein. Most days begin with two hard-boiled eggs, a glass of water, and a diet coke. My favorite mornings include a stop off at the local coffee shop for my favorite iced coffee drink! Yes, it's on my food plan! Can you believe it! Late morning I'll squeeze in my favorite snack of four vanilla wafer snack well cookies - only four points! Lunch is typically a salad with carrots, fat-free Italian dressing, and either grilled chicken or a lean cuisine meal (the points are conveniently listed on the package). An afternoon snack of fat-free cookies is worth four points, while dinner consists of a huge salad with tomatoes, carrots, fat-free dressing, and grilled chicken! While this is a typical day, a weekend day may include a trip to my favorite fast food chicken restaurant for a six-point sandwich and a diet coke! The secret is to be sure to write EVERYTHING down! It's almost like a checkbook! The days that I don't write down my food selections may sometimes find me in 'overdrawn' status!

My daily routine also consists of a visit to the company gym! I have progressed from walking thirty minutes to running four miles five days a week. I like to take off at least two days.

Alternating my routine is necessary so that I don't get too bored! Sometimes I'll run two miles outside on the track, then two inside OR I'll run two miles on the treadmill inside then do twenty minutes on the elliptical machine. Also key is my frame of mind. It is the determining factor as to whether or not a good workout will happen! If I tell myself that I don't really want to be there, then guess what - my heart isn't in it and my workout routine for that day suffers. This is why music works well for me! I won't leave home without my Walkman! Fun and upbeat music keeps my pace going, and before you know it your done. Forty minutes or four miles is my daily workout goal.

Exercise *has* played a key role in my weight loss. Keep in mind that I started out very, very slow. If you start out too hard you might hurt yourself and quickly lose the motivation you had when you started! My daily lifestyle is reflective of some type of workout, whether it is running, biking, or walking, I had added exercise to my way of life. I look at it as if it were a survival need such as air, water or food. Once you add this routine as a part of your day you'll find your mind is clearer and the everyday stresses are much easier to deal with!

My workout is not always an easy one! There are days I push myself to finish the last half-mile. Little things motivate me, another runner giving me the thumbs up sign, trying to keep up with Pete, Gary, or Steig, visualizing my best friend & boyfriend Jory coaching me on at the last half mile, or just thinking about how great life is and how good I feel! These are just a few inspiring things to keep me going through some of my workouts!

My children are also a huge part of my life. I'll never forget the time we celebrated one of Christopher's first soccer goals. He was five at the time and driving the team's soccer ball to the goal, only problem was the goal was our team's! He kicked that ball with such force! You can imagine the screaming that was coming from the sidelines! It was then, just after he scored against our team when I caught the look on his face as he looked at me. He was SO proud! He was gleaming! His joy spilled into my heart _ I was so proud of him. I had to show him by screaming, "WAY TO GO SON!" The other parents looked at me as if I had lost my mind! I didn't want to be the one responsible for taking any pride away from my child! The power of praise is evident! More importantly, the lack of that praise is just as powerful. Why do we look at the bad grades first on the report card? Acknowledge the good grades first, the soccer ball going into the goal, then discuss ways together to correct the situation. We only have one chance with them, make it count! They learn to celebrate life's obstacles as you would. YOU are their role model. YOU are the one that is looked up to! YOU can make a difference!

Surround yourself with positive energy/people

Choosing to celebrate the good days and bad days is something I must consciously do every single day. Many of the obstacles have been obvious, some not. The obvious obstacles have been the food choices I've made, the frame of mind I choose everyday, and most importantly the people I surround myself with.

Attitude is infectious. I come to work most mornings energized! I wake up with the thought that life is short, passion prevails, and it's always about the people! I experience a positive power exuberating from those within close proximity when I share my joy! I see more smiles, hear more laughter, and sense a true 'well-being' with those whose path I cross.

I must be honest with you. I do not always have the 'cheerleader' spirit! The day I came back to work after helping my boyfriend, Jory, move to Arizona ranked rock bottom on my energy chart! How could I come in the office and spread true joy when all I felt like doing was crying! There was a dull, quiet energy invading not only my office space, but also with those that I work with! Amazing, while I was able to see direct results from sharing previous joy, I was also able to see how people were affected by my current sadness! I had to do an immediate 360-degree turn and find Teresa again! Once I was able to find true Teresa, the laughter, joy, and smiles returned immediately!

I once heard from one of my closest friends, DeLynn, that, and I believe her Father told her this, you can count your true friends on one hand. Ok, let's see, Jory, Kier, DeLynn, Larry, Janis, and Mark (I know that's six!) are part of my heart and soul. You know what? Every person I just named knows exactly where he or she stands with me. The love I have for each of these people is evident, yet separate with each person. Larry don't freak out; I love you like a brother!

I've known DeLynn the longest of each of the five. DeLynn was my big sister in the Chi Omega sorority in Laramie, Wyoming. DeLynn and I had so much fun! She has this infectious smile, incredible persona, and is just a good human being. In fact, my daughter Sydneys' middle name is DeLynn. I'm smiling at this very moment - that's what thinking of DeLynn does for me. She is one of the most positive/supportive people I've ever had in my life! What's funny is the fact that while in school together, we were on so many fad diets together! When we faced a setback with whatever diet we were on, we recognized it immediately and rewarded ourselves by driving to Baskin Robbins for our favorite ice cream!

Are you thinking of someone in your life that brings a smile to your face? If not, try to. Shut your eyes and think about a time in your life when you were genuinely happy. What memory jumps out first? Were you a child, adult? Was the memory a recent one? Was the person you were thinking about in this memory? Sometimes we are in such a hurry to live life that we forget to really live life. My most recent memory was just last month! It was Kier's college graduation celebration. Her parents have a trampoline in their back yard. It's been years since I've jumped on one. I mustered up the courage to climb on this huge toy, and when I did WAHOO what fun! I laughed so hard I cried! Why didn't I do this sooner? Then my boyfriend, Jory, joined in; he was having just as much fun as I was! I can see that day as if it were yesterday! The kids loved it! They were so proud that their Mom could do a front flip!

Recognizing who or what the *'positive'* energy/people are in your life is imperative! It is also very true when it comes to recognizing the *'negative'* energy/people. Understanding that this energy is also there will be a contributing factor to achieving your goals! The negative energy could come in the form of an acquaintance, friend, or family member just to name a few. Their intentions may be good, but seeing you fail rather than succeed may bring a good feeling to their being. I wish I could tell you I had the ingredient that would get their buy-in; I don't. I do still care for those that didn't share in my dreams; I have distanced myself from them. I've been able to let some of them back in my life for the simple fact that I'm stronger than I was before. I've found that I have to be quick on my feet to recognize when or if the same negativity is back. Remembering who/what is important will keep you on track. Believe it or not, having negative energy/people in my life actually made me who I am today.

You'll be shocked at what you are able to learn about yourself by living in situations that you wished had never happened! Some people can't believe I married Roy twice! I learned more about myself the second time than I did the first. Many mistakes were made. Really, is it fair to call life's lessons mistakes?

Especially when you learn so much from them? I learned things about myself that I carry over to the relationship I'm currently in now. I know most of my good attributes, but more importantly I learned the ones that I don't want to repeat. I've seen what kind of pain is caused by my past actions or by the words that I've chosen. I don't ever want to inflict that kind of pain onto another person again. I'm not able to promise a perfect relationship, I am able to understand what is important, what's not, and when to say, "I'm sorry". If I had not lived this lesson then who would I be today?

Believe! Believe In Yourself!

Believing in yourself is directly related to what your visual or vision of your goal(s) are. You have to believe that you *will* reach your goals. Believing that you will reach your goals takes *your* vision, your buy-in and most importantly - *your* action! Other people may have a role in you achieving or succeeding your vision, but it's takes you believing in yourself that will enroll them!

You may have to verbally tell yourself that *you* can do it! Sometimes when I'm running the last half-mile of a four mile run, I want to just stop and walk! In my mind I remember a key moment in my life when someone who believes in me almost more than I do ran a 5k race with me, then came back to coach me in the last half mile! That moment is forever engraved in my memory, and heart. So, when I am training and find myself wanting to stop and walk, I remember my *'Jory'* moment and I'm able to finish! It's very easy to let the self-doubt seep in, push it out! See yourself wherever it is you are going. See yourself in the job you are seeking, as the coach you want to be, in the size you know you can be! Scared of succeeding? You already know I am! Succeeding involves certain risks and many challenges. It's not going to be easy, but that's what makes it so rewarding!

Let's talk. I want you to take your mind off my story and focus on your story. Have you been able to relate to any of the situations I've been talking about? If so, take a minute and write down some of the goals you have in mind. Write down *every* goal that comes to mind. Then go a step further and write what *action steps* you will need to do in order to achieve your goal(s). Also be sure to note what *setbacks* you might experience along the way just so you are that much more prepared! A setback could be a holiday, a birthday, or vacation, just to name a few. If you recognize what future setbacks you may have ahead of you, you can plan how you will handle those setbacks now! In other words *you* can change the future! Is this a movie or what? It is, and *you* are the headliner. This life is *your* moment, *your* time to shine, to make the most out of every learning lesson here on this grand planet!

When you find yourself in the midst of a setback try to be very conscious of how you will react to the situation. In other words, what behavior do you exhibit? Realize how much of an impact you have on not only your life, rather those people that surround you. YOU have the power to choose your behavior, and to affect other peoples' lives. Do you have a positive or negative impact? Think hard about some previous setbacks and what the end result was. Think about what you learned about yourself, and others. What would have worked better? What didn't work so well? File this information in your memory for the next time that you are in this or a similar situation, and think about how your might choose a different outcome.

I've mentioned just a few people that inspire me. These people are energetic, positive, kind people that are necessary in my life! It's always about "the people". We meet so many people everyday! As you cross another person's path consider yourself lucky to have been in their life/their movie for a brief moment! How are you able to contribute to their movie? Is it with a smile when you see that their day may be getting of to a rocky start? Is it buying the person's lunch behind you, just because? Is it realizing that the policeman that pulled you over for speeding is just doing his job? It's give and take, take and give. How do you want to be remembered? How can you make a difference? I say, "Pass it on"!

Before I say goodbye, I want to thank you for taking the time to read my story. My hope is that somewhere along the way you were able to relate to something I said, and to know that you are not alone. Believe that you are able to live your life as you choose to, and that you will achieve your goal(s)!

Thank you to everyone in my life that has believed in me!

Thank you to the Man up above, the angels that pick me up everyday, and the people I hold closely in my heart! Remember to be true to yourself, and remember, "Life is short. . . Passion Prevails. . .and it's Always About The People!"

Love,
Teresa!

Teresa Bower
Manager of Organizational Development, BNSF

Assess your General Christian Quotient

Using the scale below, please rank your response to the following statements.
4(Strongly Agree) 3(Agree) 2(Disagree) 1(Strongly Disagree)

——— 1. There is an Almighty God who Loves His creation unconditionally

——— 2. This same Almighty God desires an intimacy with His creation

——— 3. Ultimate human joy and peace can be found in the pursuit and the development of this relationship

——— 4. This spiritual relationship is offered through love and obtained by faith

——— 5. Only when you have experienced the joylessness of material possession, broken heartedness, physical decay, and emotional deprivation does the deep meaning and the significance of this divine relationship emerge as a necessity for an abundant life

——— 6. This relationship can only be fully enjoyed by emptying yourself of hate, pride, selfishness, arrogance, and violence and intellectual idolatry

——— 7. The Almighty wants to empower you to live out the core principles of Dunamis: Love, Joy, Peace, Patience, Kindness, Goodness, Faithfulness, Humility and Discipline, as we interface with one another

——— 8. For over 2000 years humanity *through greed, ambition and narcissism* has transformed the offer of a divine spiritual relationship into a humanistic philosophy; an ethnocentric, ideological culture; a stoic, rigid, legalistic, institution and a commercialized, profitable ecclesiastical, enterprise

I have read Dunamis and I think it provides a great foundation for success. This concept could not have come at a better time due to the events of 9/11. As a high school senior many of my classmates and I are thinking about what is truly important in life and trying to figure out the meaning of life. This book will inspire you and will give you hope, it can also give you a sense of direction, helping you to find the passion to follow your dreams and to realize your goals. By reading and applying Dunamis you will realize it is never too late to live your dreams. Realizing your potential is only half the battle; the real challenge is to maximize your potential and Dunamis will assist with that effort.

Jason Robinson (J-Rob)
High School Senior • Class of 2003
Strongsville, Ohio

A refreshing, common-sense approach to leadership excellence through constant gathering of new information, developing talent, overcoming adversity and building character."

Dave Tolle,
Assistant Vice President BNSF

Ron Archer is one of the most dynamic speakers I've had the opportunity to hear. His message on Dunamis Leadership is insightful compelling and motivational. He is truly one of the gifted speakers/authors of this era.

Craig Hill,
Vice President Engineering and Mechanical
BNSF Fort Worth Texas